Food Obsessed: What

How Talking to God Helped

To contact the author, email: rivkafuchscoach@gmail.com

ISBN: 978-0-9969587-3-8

Printed in the United States of America

Table of Contents

Foreward

Chapter ~ 1 ~
 "First Sin"   Page 7

Chapter ~ 2 ~
 "From the Depths"   Page 17

Chapter ~ 3 ~
 "Listening"   Page 21

Chapter ~ 4 ~
 "Pizza"   Page 25

Chapter ~ 5 ~
 "Unglorify Food".   Page 29

Chapter ~ 6 ~
 "Willing or Wanting"   Page 33

Chapter ~ 7 ~
 "Obstacles"   Page 37

Chapter ~ 8 ~
 "It's All in the Mind"   Page 49

Chapter ~ 9 ~
 "To Weigh or Not to Weigh"   Page 53

Chapter ~ 10.~
 "Focus on the Good"   Page 55

Chapter ~ 11 ~
 "Does Food Make You Happy or Sad"   Page 59

Chapter ~ 12~
 "Prayer and Food"   Page 63

Chapter ~ 13 ~
 "The Five Senses"   Page 67

Chapter ~ 14~
 "The Blame Game"   Page 73

Chapter ~ 15 ~
 "The Biggest Win"   Page 77

Chapter ~ 16 ~
 "Invisible"   Page 83

Chapter ~ 17 ~
 "Messing Up"   Page 89

Chapter ~ 18 ~
 "Psalms"   Page 93

Chapter ~ 19 ~
 "What Do I Eat"   Page 99

Chapter ~ 20 ~
 "Maintenance"   Page 113

Chapter ~ 21 ~
 "Did Someone Say Exercise"   Page 119

Chapter ~ 22 ~
 "Summing It Up"   Page 125

Afterword   Page 127

Acknowledgments   Page 131

About the Author   Page 133

I cry reading Chapter One of my first book, "Winning the Weight Loss War, How I Lost 100 Pounds for Good - And How You Can, Too." My eyes not only water, but tears pour down my face. It describes many painful moments of being overweight from childhood until I was thirty-eight years old. Now, more than thirty years later, more than 100 pounds are still off.

What were the answers to losing weight and keeping the pounds off? What tools were the most helpful? I shared the story of the many diets, types of exercise, and other effective disciplines. All helped for a while but ended up not sustaining results. Hard work for sure, but nothing was more important than the piece I didn't fully recognize. So the search continued for what would stop the insanity of my food addiction.

The missing piece in my recovery was God. I began speaking to Him, without the cushion of written words in a prayer book. If I forgot to talk to Him, I would eventually slip back into failure. The driving force to write this book is to help others relieve the depths of helplessness experienced by an addictive personality and to share how God fits into my ongoing recovery.

Speaking about my food addiction with Him led me to realize that dieting was a diversion. Eating was masking the real issues I needed to deal with in my life.

With God's help, I discovered the underlying problems that drove me to overeat. It is written in Psalms, Chapter 105, Verse 4, "Search for God and His help, look for His presence always."

Writing about God reverently and respectfully is of utmost importance. Citing Biblical sources are presented to reinforce man's dialogues with God from the beginning of time. There are religious teachings that when God is revealed in the world, the Messiah will come. As it says in Song of Songs, Chapter 2, Verse 9, "Behold, He was standing behind our wall, watching us through windows, and peering through the lattices." God is depicted as if in hiding, waiting for us to seek Him out. He is not ignoring us but giving us the opportunity to find Him and engage Him in our lives.

God is waiting for us to connect with Him.

Chapter ~1~

~ First Sin ~

What's God got to do with man's first sin of eating from the forbidden Tree of Knowledge? What is the connection of the proverbial apple that it could be a representation of not being able to resist when food beckons? According to the Book of Genesis, God warned Adam not to eat from only one tree in the entire garden. To help us understand food from the beginning of time, let's take a look at verses in Genesis that first mention food and the tree that bore the prohibited fruit.

On the third day of creation of the world, Chapter 1, Verse 11, "God said, 'Let the earth sprout vegetation: herbage yielding seed, fruit trees yielding fruit each after it's kind, containing its own seed on the earth.' And it was so." Verse 12 continues, "And the earth brought forth vegetation: herbage yielding seed after its kind, and trees yielding fruit, each containing its seed after its kind." If read quickly, you might miss this subtle change and think the two verses are repetitious. The first verse simply states the earth sprouted vegetation. The second verse says God commands the earth to sprout and the earth obeys. As you continue to read, keep this thought in the back of your mind.

On the sixth day of creation, God creates the first human being. Chapter 1, Verse 27, "So God created man in His image, in the image of God He created him; male and female He created them." God then commands man in Chapter 1, Verse 28, "Be fruitful and multiply, fill the earth and subdue it; and rule over the fish of the sea, bird of the sky, and every living thing that moves on the earth." Chapter 1, Verse 29, "God said, Behold, I have given to you all herbage yielding seed that is on the surface on the earth, and every tree that has seed-yielding fruit: it shall be yours for food." The word food appears for the first time, instructing man to eat in verse 29.

It's curious to note that the Hebrew word for seed, "zerah", is repeated many times in verses, 11, 12 and 29. Scholars have taught us there are no extra words in the Bible. However, not only is the word seed used many times, it is used as double language, "seed, seed." A synonym for the word seed is root. The definition is "the basic cause, source, or origin of something." We plant seeds which sprout and become food. Could food be the "root" beginning, the basic cause, of all taboo temptations in this world? Could it be alluding that food will be a huge struggle for mankind and a representation of all improper desires that one is expected to overcome? Only a few verses later we get into big trouble with food. Death was the consequence from eating something that was forbidden (Chapter 3, Verse 19, "...and to dust shall you return) .

Chapter 2, Verse 8, is the first mention of the famous Garden of Eden. "Hashem Elokim planted a garden in Eden, to the east, and placed there the man whom

He had formed." Throughout Chapter One, God was referred to simply as God. Starting in Chapter 2, God is referred to as "Hashem Elokim...." There are many names of God, including "Hashem," but the name "Elohim" indicates a God of judgment. Why is "Hashem Elokim" being used now and not used before God commanded the earth? Remember, when the earth was commanded, it immediately obeyed. Is this preparing us for the God who will need to use his authority to judge and punish man?

Chapter 2, Verse 9 is the first verse to mention the pleasure of seeing food and the tree man was forbidden to eat from. "Every tree pleasing to the eye and good for food; also the Tree of Life in the midst of the garden, and the Tree of Knowledge of Good and Bad." A few verses later man is told he can eat from every tree in the garden except for one. Verse 16, "And Hashem God commanded the man, saying, 'Of every tree of the garden you may freely eat;' Verse 17, "but of the Tree of Knowledge of Good and Bad, you must not eat thereof; for on the day you eat of it, you shall surely die." Sounds like a setup? Imagine being told to enter a bakery, see the scrumptious cakes and then be told, "By the way. You can't have any."

Here comes man's first sin and the interrogation. Chapter 3, second half of Verse 11, "Have you eaten from the tree from which I have commanded you not to eat?" Can we read between the lines? "Have you given into your cravings? Have you disregarded the laws I have given to mankind?"

Does Adam really desire the fruit? On the surface one might suppose he is hungry. However, in psychology, this may be termed the "presenting" issue, the problem we see on the surface. Adam had a craving for something much greater than a bite of a juicy, red apple. Adam was led to believe that if he ate from the Tree of Knowledge of Good and Bad, he would become as great as God. This led him to question if something was missing in his life. Could there be a connection between emptiness and eating to fill a void?

Understanding this story may unravel some of the mystery behind our desire to eat even when we are not hungry or conscious that we are harming ourselves by eating too much food.

Overeating is a habit we develop over time as we wind our way through our unmanageable lives. Eating what we crave seems to satisfy us. In the moment, our goal to relieve hunger is accomplished. Feeling physically full obviously doesn't satisfy anything other than physical hunger. Somewhere along the way, our wires got crossed. We substitute food as a panacea for difficulties and lack in all areas. Addictions come in all packages; food, drugs, alcohol, gambling or shopping.

It's a conundrum that with more advances in technology and so many inventions that appear to save us time, our lives are more harried than ever. Obesity is steadily on the rise as a result of our stress-induced, faster-paced lives combined with the advent of fast food, take-out, and an increased number of meals eaten in restaurants. Chewing has been proven to reduce anxiety. Hence, food does calm our nerves.

We need instruction and boundaries. We know there are many things we can have and do within limits. This works for society and works for dieting, too! We can't eat without abandon and not expect to gain weight just as we can't run amuck in society and expect order to just happen.

Look at the world today. Glance back at the story of Adam. Not restraining oneself may wreak havoc. Is there a connection between Adam not restraining an urge and consequences? Is it possible that overindulgence in any of the aforementioned addictions causes the turmoil we see in the world today? Adam did not resist the apple and we know that did not end well.

One purpose of the Old Testament is to provide us with solutions to the situations we face in life; a blueprint to help navigate our lives. Problems such as sibling rivalry, jealousy, kingdoms warring with each other, stealing, and murder; anything and everything one can experience is touched upon in one way or another. Is there any hint to the cravings for food and ultimately not being able to resist? Certainly, the story of Adam and Eve exhibits just that scenario. Are there other subtle hints, cloaked in mystery elsewhere in the Bible?

Going back to the second chapter in Genesis, Chapter 2, Verse 2, states, "By the seventh day God completed His work which He had done. Verse 3 continues,

"God blessed the seventh day and sanctified it because on it He abstained from all His work which God created to make." As farfetched as this may seem, the root letters of the Hebrew word for work, are the same as the word that means food. Maybe it's my insanity with food speaking, but seeing these words juxtaposed in the same sentence jumped out at me. Common day language for overcoming compulsive overeating is to abstain. Interestingly, the word used here for 'work' is not the commonly used word for 'work.' Summing it up, we abstain from work, just as we should abstain from food by not overindulging. I believe there is a message beneath the surface here. When we sanctify anything, it is important to stop, step back, and take in what we have created. To truly enjoy, is giving the experience space to take it all in slowly. The same with food; after all the shopping, preparing and cooking - take the time to stop and offer a prayer for the privilege of having food on the table. Instead of harried rushing through a meal, take the time to truly think about the taste, the nourishment and the pleasure. Only by stopping and abstaining from a feeding frenzy can we truly enjoy our meals.

Another thought is that this sentence is referring to the day of rest, to the seventh day of the week, the Sabbath. There are three festive meals to honor the day; some even have the practice of a fourth special meal when the Sabbath ends. The Sabbath is considered a holiday in the Jewish religion. Think now of the secular holidays around the world and what do we think? Food! How much anxiety is there trying not to gain weight over a holiday or even the

12

entire holiday season? Think about the fact that these are usually one day occurrences that include one meal. Now go back to the Sabbath. Three or four meals? Of course, the word abstain is there! Each meal cannot be a feast. The way to celebrate and honor this day is to have special food, not necessarily an abundance of food. Jumping ahead to Exodus, Chapter 20, Verses 8 - 14, we are instructed to remember the Sabbath. The following verses, mentioning the Sabbath again, are enumerated in six of the Ten Commandments. The fifth Commandment is to honor your parents. Interestingly enough the reward for observing this commandment is a long life. The reward for eating in a healthful manner is also longevity. The next five commandments all begin with the word, "No." Perhaps it is stretching interpretations quite a bit, but on a very simple level, "No!, Do not do any of these things that will harm you nor cause punishment." Overeating is certainly harmful on many levels, physically and emotionally.

What are we to learn from the story of Adam and Eve? So much misery came into the world because Adam ate the apple. Could it be that we rectify Adam's sin every time we are faced with food but we resist?

What if every single time we see, feel, taste, touch and desire to a degree beyond the bounds of normal, we bring some modicum of damage to the world? What if every shopping binge, large food consumption, too many alcoholic drinks, etc., brings disappointment to God? God sure was disappointed in Adam's choice, so are we any different? Are all those times of overindulgence chipping away at an ideal society?

Were we given this challenge to undo Adam's sin? We are all here for a purpose and have different roles to accomplish in the world. Interpretations of the Old Testament have taught us that once Adam and Eve ate from the tree, mankind was then infused with evil impulses. We have the opportunity to negate these through self-discipline. Could one extrapolate from this that curbing the appetite for food may lead to a person's betterment overall? Are food addicts specially chosen by God to rectify the Original Sin?

If you thought for a moment that every time you resist improper eating the world would revert to how it existed before the sin, would you be more on board with tackling your cravings knowing your efforts would remove illness, death and toil? If you felt you could bring the world to its final pristine destination, would that make it easier to put food into its proper place?

Moderation is a virtue. When do we cross the line between engaging in this world in a healthy way and when does it become more than what God wants us to be, do and have. Every one of us is a soul clothed in a body. Just as every person appears different on the outside, every invisible soul is just as unique. Each distinctive soul is equipped with the tools necessary to fulfill its life's mission. Each mission is multi-faceted and specific to that soul. What may appear to be indulgence for one soul, may be the baseline for another. Each of us has a threshold for what is excessive and for another, just barely enough.

Scriptures show us that right from the beginning, God is talking to us and we are talking to Him. Somewhere along the line, we no longer directly hear Him. Going forward in the Scriptures, only the holiest of people had this privilege, albeit in a cloaked manner.

Even though we can't hear God, He does want our attention and our words. Introducing daily conversations with Him has helped countless people overcome addictions. Twelve-step programs have taught us to rely on Him. If you have not yet tried this avenue to help with dieting, it is time to begin.

How does one begin to talk to God? The next chapter will introduce this ancient, powerful practice.

Chapter ~ 2 ~

~ From the Depths ~

"From the depths I called to You G-d. O Lord hear my voice, may Your ears be attentive to the sound of my pleas." Psalms 130

I was desperate to lose weight, but every diet failed. Just when I resigned to being obese for the rest of my life, God placed me in a group meeting. It was foreign to me that they were discussing speaking to God directly; and about food, no less. As much religious observance as I had, it never occurred to me to talk to God other than reciting words from a prayer book. Admittedly, I realized I was stuck in my childhood view of God as being distant, strict, scary and most of all, unapproachable. Listening to them made me wonder if God wanted to hear directly from me, *in my own words.* Thanks to this group, I began speaking to God, albeit in a very shallow way. Only when I was about to overeat I would call out, "God help me!" It did work sometimes but not all the time. Success was attributed mostly to the the 12-Step program combined with diet and exercise.

Even though I was still keeping off a lot of weight, the foundation of the struggle was still there. I slipped too frequently seeking comfort. The talking to

God thing was still in the background. As God would have it, I was drawn to classes on improving my spirituality. In particular, the idea of talking to God in an intimate fashion fascinated me. For years, I wanted to learn Jewish meditation. I read there were two types. Hisbonenus, which in very simple terms, is quieting the mind with Godly images, is what I focused on. This had no effect on healing my compulsive overeating. The other type, called Hisbodedus, was truly what I needed to heal but never got around to exploring.

Many years passed before I had the opportunity to learn Hisbodedus. God places in our lives what we need when we are ready for it. Hisbodedus is the Jewish term for talking to God; just you and Him alone having a conversation. The Holy Rabbi who introduced us to this practice is Rebbe Nachman of Breslov. He was born on April 4, 1772, in the town Medzhybizh, Ukraine. To this day, hundreds of thousands of people travel to Uman to pray at his grave. He brought many spiritual teachings to the world but his main message was, "Talk to God!" He advised talking to God as we would to a true, dear friend.

I had the privilege to learn Rebbe Nachman's teachings with my spiritual leader, Rav Moshe Weinberger. December 24, 2020, Rav Weinberger started teaching a book called, "Before You, I Pour Out My Conversations," based on Rebbe Nachman's advice. The book discusses how, when, and every single angle of how to converse with God. To my astonishment, in the class I joined on that day, the book started the topic of food and not eating in a proper way. At that moment, I felt God *was speaking directly to me!* I always considered food an

18

area far removed from anything to discuss with God. This book proved to me that the topic of food *is* a huge deal and worth discussing. It explained it is not simply that a person doesn't have willpower. It comes from a very deep place and is a problem that needs to be addressed. The fact that it was written about in the 1700s shows it has been an issue for a very long time.

Hisbodedus involved a huge learning curve; I second-guessed whether this was for the average person like me or reserved for holy people on much higher spiritual and religious levels. However, I wanted so much to connect to God on a deeper level. I persisted and exerted myself beyond my comfort level.

I felt like an amateur and doubted I was doing this talking-to-God thing correctly. Soon after an acquaintance called and asked if I was interested in learning Hisbodedus together on Zoom with a group of women. I jumped at the chance as I was drawn to this talking to God stuff, as a magnet to a piece of metal.

I was in awe of approaching God in such a direct way. Only through learning the book, "In Forest Fields: A Unique Guide to Personal Prayer," by Rabbi Shalom Arush, with this group of women, did I become less intimidated. We delved into the definition of the word Hisbodedus. The root of the Hebrew word means to be alone, connoting this practice to being alone with God; a one-on-one conversation about everything, including the most mundane.

We learned to imagine picking up the phone and pouring our hearts out - to talk about anything and everything. You never have to worry about your innermost secrets and thoughts being divulged. What makes this even better is knowing God already *knows* all your thoughts. You can talk to Him without ever having to feel shame. He created everything you experience so nothing you share will shock Him.

An "aha" moment was realizing my food struggles were God's way of bringing me closer to Him. Speaking to Him plays the foremost role in keeping my weight consistent. It took years to come to this point, but as time went on, it became natural to talk to Him as opposed to my initial reluctance. The food cravings diminished, rarely rearing their ugly head.

You too can have this wonderful relationship with God. Keep talking to Him until your unhealthy desire for food goes away. Discuss in great detail where you want help. Talk about the challenges you need to overcome. Ask for help and be very specific about what your needs are. Have continued gratitude as the desire for food slips away, knowing the help is coming from God. Keep talking until it becomes a habit and most of all, till you see the magic happening.

Pretty soon the voice that used to scream at you, "Eat!," becomes just a whisper and will be drowned out by your voice saying, "Thank you God for all Your help."

Chapter ~ 3 ~

~ Listening ~

The more you speak to God on a regular basis, the more He will manifest in your life. You will notice answers to questions you have had right in front of you all along. Never before thought of solutions will come your way for unresolved problems. At first you may shrug them off as coincidence, but eventually it will be evident that God is speaking directly to you.

How does one distinguish between what came from God and what we figured out on our own? The differences are subtle at first, but increased frequency will have you know. You will start to see patterns and the answers from God will come closer to the time you asked for help. Opening your eyes, heart and mind will allow this to happen.

My craziness with food lasted for so many years. If you are not in the shoes of a food addict, it is hard to imagine the struggle going on in the mind over what to eat. Even when I committed my meals to writing, I would inevitably grab too much of the wrong foods, failing to stick to what I had planned, until I learned to ask God for help.

"Good morning God. Believe it or not, I don't remember what is best for me to eat today. Guide me. What should I have for breakfast? Should I even eat breakfast? I am not hungry. Should I wait for lunch today to have my first meal?" I then noticed a piece of paper on the floor, wondering what it was. It was the food plan I had written down the night before that I had completely forgotten about. God answered me.

A compulsive overeater's brain is so messed up when it comes to food, that even the most intelligent person becomes a fool. How I struggled to eat normally at a restaurant for many, many years. Before I went I promised myself I would not touch the bread basket and then devoured it all every single time. I promised I wouldn't order dessert and then found myself taking the last bite of the chocolate cake. A food addict literally blanks. You look back and again beat yourself up for failing. It's embarrassing to admit how many years this went on until I had this connection with God. Knowing what to do came easily going forward. I could not recognize the person I used to be. I understood that I never would have figured this out by myself. God was truly feeding me calorie-free solutions.

Listening yet more closely led me to have the space to recognize it wasn't food I needed. Again, God guiding me. When He stopped the binge, it gave me time to reflect. When thoughts of food began to flood my mind it was important to check my feelings at this point. Was anything bothering me? Was I pushing down feelings I needed to address? The first few times we do this it is common to blank, not to have any idea of the emotions we are actually experiencing. "Nope. Nothing bothering me now. I just want food." I became so accustomed to soothing myself with food that I fooled myself and resisted recognizing what was upsetting me. Dr. John Sarno, a well-respected doctor and author on back pain, explains in his books that our brains use pain to distract us from experiencing negative emotions. Some unknowingly choose physical pain; his books specifically address back pain. In my case, I chose to numb myself with food, rather than deal with unmanageable feelings. My turning to food, as painful and difficult as that was, replaced dealing with real issues. Sometimes I wish I would have chosen that route; backaches and not food. But that was not what God chose for me. It's a vicious cycle. I ate to ease the stress and became more stressed than to begin with because of the binge. I had not been cognizant in the throes of bingeing to understand I was diverting my mind from the truth of what was bothering me. I had no idea that chewing temporarily relieved stress and the sensation of being physically full filled my emotional emptiness.

During my search for learning how to communicate with God, I discovered that deep inside my soul was longing for Him. I had a hole that needed to be filled. I was so blocked and immersed in self-pity, that I couldn't see straight. The intensity was there for me to be in contact with Him in a deep, intimate way. Think about the couples you know that have the best marriages. They are the ones texting throughout the day, just checking in to see how their spouse is doing. Having this same frequency of communication with God also bespeaks a higher level of connection.

Stop, take a deep breath, and let God get to work. Ask for advice and then let thoughts just come to you. It's similar to not being able to retrieve a word and best trying not to. Calm will take over and that alone will help you choose the foods that are best for each meal. Are you feeling stressed? Talk to God about it. Wait for Him to soothe you. You also experience a newfound sense of safety that permeates your being. Even problems I used to get upset over, I look back and am stunned that I ever let them bother me.

Not to be misunderstood, it is important to differentiate between getting the answers to overcome addictive eating and fixing the problems in your life. The problems that led to stuffing our faces may stay unresolved. Giving them over to God may be the best situation as long as the end goal is eliminating compulsive overeating. Accept that in God's eyes, everything we experience has a purpose and shapes us into who we become, *depending on our choices,* and that may be the only answer. Listen to what you can do to replace stuffing your problems down with cookies and cakes. Listen for God's help in choosing different outlets to release pain and disappointments. Understanding that God knows best, I am in such a different place that I can remain relaxed in moments that left me so jarred in the past.

God wanted my attention. Give Him some attention and you will be rewarded with so much more, too.

Chapter ~ 4 ~

"Pizza"

Speaking to God is tantamount but other things need to be in place, too. The motto, "God helps those that help themselves," emphasizes the importance of self-initiative. We won't get results, no matter how much we talk to God, if we don't roll up our sleeves. This is not "Splitting of the Sea" territory, (Exodus 14: 19-31); we are not relying on miracles.

Pizza and bagels were foods I thought I could never give up completely. "Are you willing to eliminate bagels and pizza?" Years ago my answer would have been a resounding and absolute, "No!" My sanity was replaced with desires that were beyond my control *at that time.* Little did I understand that the food itself was partially to blame.

The effect of white flour foods wreaked havoc with my broken metabolism, caused by decades of yo-yo dieting and bouts of bouncing between starvation diets and bingeing. Even with a normal metabolism, all carbohydrates turn into sugar once ingested. The sugar activates the brain's reward system called the mesolimbic dopamine system, sometimes referred to as the reward pathway. Dopamine is a neurohormone released by our brain that fires up the euphoric feelings. This makes us want more of the same. It becomes impossible to resist eating another portion. A vicious cycle ensues. The temporary euphoria makes us eat more, then leads to feeling depressed as the sugar levels drop. When we wake up from our stupor, we feel even worse.

The desire to let go of the food has to become greater than the desire to eat the food. The resolve to say you are ready to stop harming yourself with these foods has to be absolute. The above physiological explanations assure you that it is not completely your fault but these foods need to be eliminated. You wouldn't offer an alcoholic a drink. Why would you feed yourself self-harming foods that set you up for defeat?

The thought of never having a slice of pizza again in your life may not be something you are willing to do and neither was I. For *now,* that has to be the commitment. A certain amount of healing, physically and emotionally, needs to occur if certain foods will slowly be introduced back into your diet. The falsely imagined pleasure once attached to these foods has to be completely *obliterated* from your mind. Perhaps they can be reintroduced but that is a whole other discussion of when and how and only after being able to eat moderate portions without craving more.

So pray *long and hard.* I'm ashamed to say that sometimes when hitting rock bottom, I'd fall to the ground begging God for help. Those were the times I opened up completely, crying for Him to come to my rescue. God knew my struggles. God knew my cravings and insanity with food. But I now understand he wanted to hear it directly from me. Why would he need to hear it? He doesn't have needs, *I needed to connect to Him*. I began to cherish this challenge as a personal invitation to remember to visit Him.

Giving up pizza and bagels doesn't mean eating giving up all your favorite foods. It is important to pinpoint which ones set up an eating frenzy, as pizza and bagels were for me. Crazy as this sounds, I was wary of going into deprivation mode. I gave up store bought pizza completely but made a healthier option that I found very satisfying. I halved either a 100% whole wheat English muffin, or split a mini whole wheat pita bread in half. I used a few spoons of sugar-free marinara sauce and sprinkled with low-fat shredded cheese. It is important to note here that when something is taken away, a healthy alternative should be substituted. This leads to satisfaction rather than a sense of deprivation.

I sometimes wonder if subliminally something wonderful happened the first time I ate pizza. Is it more than the pizza? Is it touching upon a wonderful memory that I am trying to re-live? Or did I find it just so darn delicious and it gave me so much pleasure that I am trying to regain that once again? I'll never know.

It's not easy to have a food completely taken out of your life but it is so worth it. If you aren't able to handle it, you have to know when to give it up. Sounds almost childish but it certainly is not. Being a grown up comes with knowledge of knowing what is good for us and what is not. We know sleep is important to function properly, so we aim for as many hours a night as we need. We know physical exercise is crucial to good health and incorporate movement into our daily lives. We must create that same mindset and eliminate any foods that are difficult for us to handle. Period.

Chapter ~ 5 ~

~ Unglorify Food ~

Not sure if unglorify is a word in the dictionary but it speaks volumes to me. I glorified all the wrong foods. That combined with the portions I saw at home was a lethal combination. Add another layer of feeling deprived and that left me with a huge gaping hole. As a child, I had no coping mechanism other than to mindlessly eat. This began at such a young age that I never learned how to eat intuitively.

It started at a picnic when I was eight years old. A family friend offered a bag of potato chips and called out, "Who wants potato chips?" I declined because I wasn't hungry. He looked and me and bellowed out, "You don't look like you don't eat potato chips!" I watched children and adults around me laughing and felt shame for the first time in my life. When I went home, I remember viewing my body in horror and labeling myself fat. The sadder part is looking at pictures of myself at that age now as an adult. I wasn't skinny but I certainly wasn't fat. However, that event catapulted me into misery for the next thirty years.

I began to categorize food at the age of eight. I lumped all the foods, that magazine articles said were fattening, into one group. I denied myself all these foods all the time. We all know what happens when something is forbidden.

Look at Adam, first man. The one food he was told not to eat, he could not resist. I glorified many foods and in doing so, I craved them even more. I watched people eating bakery goods while my mouth watered. How could such a young child begin to have such an obsession with food?

By the time I was eleven years old, even healthy foods were included in my forbidden list. I never allowed myself to eat whole grains, winter squashes, brown rice or bread. I read that bananas, grapes and watermelon have way too much sugar if you want to lose weight. All these foods should have been eaten in moderation. By now you are thinking, "How did she get so fat not eating all those foods?" Withholding them led to my eating disorder. I was either starving or bingeing. I did not know any other way. I would go days with only eating iceberg lettuce because I so desperately wanted to be thin. Then true hunger would set it and it took tons of food to make up for the days of starvation.

As an adult I had to separate the good from the bad, to take my "never eat foods" list, and break it down into definitely leave these out but not those! My success in keeping weight off was to completely eliminate many unhealthy foods. Eliminating foods meant not having them in the house altogether. It was time for a pantry overhaul. Everything that I went to on auto-mode when a binge would start was given away or thrown in the garbage. My health had to be the priority.

Besides the obvious offenders like chips, cakes, cookies, pizza and bagels, there were certain meals that I needed to avoid because they too would lead me to eat without abandon, such as eggplant parmesan. I was lucky that no one in my home really cared for it so it was easy to eliminate that from our dinner menu. I did not realize I made it more for myself than for anyone else. After discussions with my family, they all told me it was one of their least favorite meals, as well as any meal involving pasta. I was fortunate because the foods they liked the least were the ones I loved the most.

Fast forward about thirty years. In all those years I never ate eggplant parmesan, even though it had once been a favorite. It is one of the perfect examples of eliminating is easier than having just a small portion. I had gotten to the point where I just never craved the old favorites forgetting about them completely.

A friend ordered eggplant parmesan when we went out to lunch. I wasn't thinking, "Oh, poor me. I never eat my favorite foods anymore." I watched her pick up forkful by forkful with the melted cheese oozing on her plate. I even thought, "It doesn't even look appealing. It's swimming in oily, fried and breaded eggplant. That no longer appeals to me!"

However, one day without any explanation, I started thinking I would order that dish for dinner. In the restaurant, instead of ordering my usual salad and grilled protein, I ordered a salad and eggplant parmesan. In addition, I ordered it served over zucchini spirals instead of over spaghetti, which were the two options on the menu. Pretty good choice, the zucchini, rewarding myself mentally for not having ordered it on a bed of spaghetti. The food addict is notorious for excusing oneself with momentary loss of sanity. In the past, I would have justified the spaghetti by rationalizing, "I'm going off my diet. I may as well order the spaghetti, too."

I took one bite and was very disappointed! It didn't taste anywhere as phenomenal as I had remembered. It proved to be once again, that when you eat right for a long enough time, your taste buds don't even enjoy foods that you once found appealing. I didn't do my usual wrap-it-up and give it to someone because I was wasting money. If it is not healthy enough for me to eat, I wouldn't consider giving it to anyone else.

That experience reminded me of how good the healthy food I eat tastes. Clean foods are what I fill my plate up with now. It also reminded me of how I glorified the foods I gave up in order to lose weight. The memory was with rose-colored glasses, just like a lost love. Had the love been so great, you wouldn't have lost it.

So stop pining for and glorifying the fattening foods you think taste great and also for the ones that actually do; because thin and healthy tastes much better.

Chapter ~ 6 ~

~ Willing or Wanting ~

Why would anyone in their right mind allow themselves to become overweight? I am asking *myself* the question. Not just overweight but downright obese. So many in this unfortunate club are intelligent people who function fabulously well in every other area of their lives. I honestly believe their lives would have been exponentially better had they not had the weight on their minds of being overweight on the scale.

It is all-consuming. What will I eat today? What will breakfast, lunch and dinner look like? How many calories a day should I be eating? What is my healthy BMI? How many calories are in an orange? How often can I eat carbohydrates and lose weight? How often can I eat carbohydrates and maintain my weight? What the heck is a carbohydrate? Which foods have carbohydrates in them? What's the difference between a healthy carbohydrate and a non-healthy carbohydrate?

Let's continue the insanity. Should I weigh and measure my food? Is it more accurate to use measuring spoons and cups or should I be weighing on a food scale? Which brand food scale is the most accurate? Perhaps it is better to learn to eyeball food portions or perhaps it is not. Which diet would have me losing weight the fastest? There are hundreds of dietary theories. Hundreds, if not thousands, of people I could follow on Social Media to get advice from. Whom should I follow? Whose advice would really work? Should I use a weight-loss app? Should I go to see a private nutritionist? Should I go to a group setting weight loss group? Should I try a fasting program under a doctor's supervision or a hospital?

Need I continue the questions that roll around in the mind of an overweight person? I am not exaggerating above. How could they accomplish their best lives when they have all these extraneous thoughts in the back of their minds? If not constant nor consciously aware of them, they are certainly lurking there.

Willpower. I never really understood the exact definition of that word or how it related to being able to resist food. "Control exerted to do something or restrain impulses." Here is a sentence to show how the word is commonly used, "Most of our bad habits are due to laziness or lack of willpower."

I don't have a problem with the definition but I most certainly have a problem with the sentence used to describe its meaning. Laziness? I dare say laziness is most probably not true for most people wanting to lose weight! Neither have we wasted any time going to weight loss programs, weighing and measuring our food, creating shopping lists upon shopping lists, perusing recipes galore, researching or looking up calories for every morsel we have put in our mouths, driven to support groups and so much more! Anyone who has ever tried to lose weight may not necessarily fit into the first half of this definition. The second half 'lack of willpower' also rubs me the wrong way. The word lack here just makes me bristle! Lack is what brought us to desire food more than the average person in the first place! The definition of lack is "the state of being without or not having enough of something." Perhaps a lack of attention, a lack of love, a lack of success, etc... may be the driving force for overeating. It is certainly not a lack of willpower!

The word I prefer is wantpower. One needs to want to be successful more than the drug you are going to that is creating the obstacles to your success. The drug in our context means the food, the alcohol, the shopping; whatever it is that is stopping you from reaching your goals.

Look at the piece of cake calling your name. You want to eat it. However, now is the time to picture your goal in your mind. Do you want the cake or do you want to lose weight? *Which do you want more?*

A good tool is to write down on index cards, "I want to be healthy," or "I want to be slim," or "I want to weigh _____." When that cake beckons, now is the time to whip out those index cards and read them! To achieve any of those goals, the cake has to go, straight into the garbage.

In Genesis, 22:1-19, God commands Abraham to slaughter his only son Isaac, the son born to him after decades of his wife Sarah not being able to conceive. Imagine waiting till you are one hundred years old to have a child. Think we have it tough deciding if we want to eat a cookie? Yet, Abraham did not hesitate

to fulfill God's directive. Can we say Abraham was using his willpower to listen

to God? Abraham used wantpower. His overriding desire and firm choice was

his greater love of God. Your commitment to yourself must be realized in firm

decisions to want your goal more than a piece of cake.

When you think you want that piece of cake, whip out that card. Which do you

want more? The cake or one of the goals on your card? If you want the cake

more at that moment, then eat it. But eat it without guilt. Enjoy it and don't

let it derail you from getting right back on your healthy eating plan. If you want

to achieve your goals sooner, your choice would be to not eat the cake. Which

do you *want more?* The cake or achieving your goal? Use your wantpower to

make a choice that will bring you to your goal.

Chapter ~ 7 ~

~ Obstacles ~

Talking to God is certainly the primary healing tool. However, there are behavioral and environmental habits we must change in order to win this battle. Here are common obstacles that lead to poor eating habits:

1- Overthinking food

2 - Not planning ahead

3 - Eating standing up

4 - Not eating at a kitchen or dining room table

5 - Eating in the car

6 - Mindless eating; watching a movie, reading or talking on the phone

7 - Eating too fast

8 - Taking second helpings

9 - Buying too much food

10 - Tempting food in the house

11 - Tempting foods at work

12 - Eating after dinner

13 - Social eating

Typing the above list reminded me of the herculean efforts I had in overcoming each one. Psalm 136 comes to mind. "Give thanks to God for He is good," "Give thanks to the God of the heavenly powers," "Give thanks to the Lord of the lords." The Psalm continues with twenty-three more lines beginning with the same words, "Give thanks." It is interesting that inserted between each phrase are the words, "for His kindness endures forever." This brought to mind to say the following after each obstacle, "God, thank you for helping me overcome this obstacle." Bring God into the healing of each as I know that in my case, my efforts alone would not have been enough.

Let's delve into each one:

1 - Before I returned home, thinking about the contents of my kitchen cabinets had me going straight to the pantry the minute I walked through the door. I imagined myself eating which made my mouth water and produced intense cravings. Thinking about coffee shops and ice cream stores I'd pass while doing errands became an effort not to go in and buy something. Thin people are not preoccupied with these thoughts.

Food was constantly on my mind. Before a binge I would plan walking down the aisles of the supermarket, envisioning everything I would buy. I would sheepishly say to the checkout girl, "I'm having a birthday party for one of my kids," knowing I would polish it all off by myself till I was stuffed and nauseous. If I had stopped those thoughts, I could have saved myself from bingeing. If I had spoken to God I possibly could have not entered the supermarket in the first place.

There was a war going on in my mind. Even the word bread in Hebrew has similar letters to the word war. The three root letters of the word "war" are the letters that spell the word "bread."   It really is a struggle between two opposite sides - the side of you that wants to eat right and the side of you that just wants to eat!

The next time you start thinking about the next binge or food fest or even about eating when you are not hungry, change your thoughts! Pay attention to what you are thinking. Beg God to help you shift your thoughts away from food. Think about your family, your pet, and your next project at work. Think about anything except food. Get it out of your mind. If you say "Stop! Help me", you will break the chain and redirect your thoughts away from a planned eating frenzy.

God, thank You for helping me overcome this obstacle.

2 - Not planning ahead is a must-change behavior. "Failing to plan is planning to fail." How true! Imagine coming home to an empty refrigerator. No fruits,

vegetables or lean protein available. Even if there are some healthy foods, they are neither washed or cooked.

Start with a weekly meal plan to create your supermarket list. Stick to your list and resist adding anything else. Get yourself in the habit of having boundaries. Wash your fruits and vegetables when you unpack from the supermarket. It will make food preparation for all future meals much quicker. Also, you will sooner grab that apple rather than a candy bar, which I hope you no longer keep in the house.

Eat only what is written down for every meal and snack. Keep track of what meals work and which don't. Writing it down not only keeps you on track and accountable, but there is also a lot of information. Review the meals that were satisfying. Notice which ones didn't keep you till the next meal. Another benefit is not only will it keep you from overeating, but it will help with keeping your mind off food.

God, thank You for helping me overcome this obstacle.

3 - Instead of eating the food you would have shoved mindlessly into your mouth standing up, put it in a plastic bag. At the end of the week, write down the amount of food you would have eaten standing up. It is absolutely astonishing.

Pay attention! Never allow yourself one morsel of food to enter your mouth while you are standing up. You may start protesting, arguing that this is impossible. "When I cook, I have to taste the food! Do you really expect me to take a spoonful to the table and eat it sitting down?" Actually, I don't! I don't want you to ever taste food while you are cooking. One taste leads to another and then another.

"How can you expect me to never taste while I am cooking? How will I know if I need to adjust the salt?" I think this is a pretty small price to pay for not eating hundreds if not thousands of additional calories a week. I completely leave out salt when I cook. There are salt shakers on my kitchen table. Want to add salt? Be my guest!

God, thank You for helping me overcome this obstacle.

4 - Designate areas where you will sit down and eat. These will be the only places you will eat in your home. When you limit your options of where you eat, you will also limit your options of how frequently you eat. Our brains take subtle cues and create imprints in our memories. If every time you sit on the den sofa you've been taking a snack, your brain will say, "Hey, snack time! Bring food to the den sofa!" Once again, it is mindless eating and more of a habit than anything else.

God, thank You for helping me overcome this obstacle.

5 - The number of people I see eating in their cars is astonishing. Clients admit there are more fast food containers and candy bar wrappers in their cars than they'd like to admit. Realize how many fewer calories will be consumed if you put a stop to this. Even if you picked up the family dinner and it is on the seat next to you and you are starving, do not start eating in your car. You won't faint if you wait till you get home to eat like a normal person, sitting down at a table to eat your meal.

God, thank You for helping me overcome this obstacle.

6 - How many times have you finished watching a movie and wondered how the family-sized popcorn bag became empty? How many times did you walk to the bakery to pick up muffins and a loaf of bread for the family, but discover how much was munched on before you got home? How much mindless nibbling on the bag of chips while engrossed in reading a newspaper or novel? The biggest offender is eating while talking on the phone. The shame of all these behaviors is that you probably didn't even enjoy your food because you weren't even paying attention! No more mindless eating, please.

God, thank You for helping me overcome this obstacle.

7 - Eating too fast is common in our fast-paced world. Now we are all rushing and pulled in many different directions.

Sing to the tune of the 59th Street Bride Song by Simon & Garfunkel:

Slow down you're eating too fast

You've got to make the mouthfuls last.

Just gulping down bite after bite

Your clothes will always stay tight.

Slow down you're chewing too fast

You've got to make mastication last.

The release of all the enzymes

To release nutrition does take time.

Slow down and notice your food

Does it taste great or only just good?

In the past, you'd never know

Because you weren't chewing slow.

You've slowed down and it feels just great

You're starting to fit into that smaller skirt.

Eating slowly makes the food last

And now you're losing weight so fast!

Just slow down! Do you polish off huge mounds of food on your plate and before you know it, your plate is empty? Eating too quickly doesn't give the brain the twenty minutes it needs to get the full signal. This sets you up for going for seconds.

God, thank you for helping me overcome this obstacle.

8 - Taking second helpings is more a habit than anything else. Normal people eat till they are no longer hungry (yes, this was also shocking to me the first time I heard that). Drink a glass of water when you finish eating. This will help you fill satisfied and prevent you from going back for more.

God, thank You for helping me overcome this obstacle.

9 - In our modern world, we buy abundantly and way more than we need. Ordering take out for dinner? Only order one meal per family member. Only buy enough non-perishables for a short period of time so you won't be

tempted to eat those extra bags of food because of the upcoming expiration date. It's a very simple formula. Buy less = eat less.

God, thank You for helping me overcome this obstacle.

10 - Keep tempting foods out of the house. It is difficult not to have your family's favorite treats in the house but your health is worth more. The next time they ask for a snack, suggest a clementine or an apple. If the complaining starts, it is time for a family meeting. Admit you can't resist certain foods; they are too tempting for you. This is a must for your success. Explain that it benefits them, too! Just because someone is slim does not mean they are necessarily healthy on the inside. The term TOFI stands for; thin outside fat inside. Just because someone is slim, it does not necessarily spare them from heart disease. You are keeping your slim family members healthier, too.

God, thank You for helping me overcome this obstacle.

11 - You have zero control over what is brought into the office. At my first job, fresh hot bagels stared me in the face every morning along with tubs of cream cheese and butter. If that wasn't enough temptation, a donut cart was wheeled in every afternoon. How do you handle situations where you do not have control? It is imperative to have healthy substitutions. Bring cut-up vegetables and keep individual portions of raw nuts or seeds, 100% whole wheat crackers, or other healthy options. Keep drinking, too! Fill up on water,

coffee, tea and flavored seltzers.

God, thank You for helping me overcome this obstacle.

12 - No eating after dinner. Period. It is possible to lose weight by only changing this one habit. Dinner should hold anyone till bedtime. It is unhealthy to have your body digest food while you sleep. Sleep is the time to rejuvenate your cells and reset many functions. Once again, take that food you were about to eat after dinner and put it in a bag. You will be astonished at how many thousands of calories were not eaten.

God, thank You for helping me overcome this obstacle.

13 - Social settings lead to mindless eating. While you are conversing with friends it is easy to lose track of how many chips you have eaten from the bowl. If you are having dinner in someone's home, food is usually served family style. How is it possible *not* to take seconds when the food is right in front of you? The strategy here is not to come hungry. Eat a filling salad or yogurt before you arrive. Plan to only sit when you do eat and be mindful of every bite you put into your mouth. Keeping your hands occupied is also helpful. When I attend a wedding smorgasbord, I keep a glass of seltzer in one hand and my cell phone in the other. I made it impossible to take food. Changing my mindset also helped. I focused on the conversations and the connection with friends.

God, thank You for helping me overcome this obstacle

Depending on how many of these self-sabotaging habits you currently engage in, it can seem quite insurmountable to overcome one, let alone all of them. Remember to be kind to yourself. Do not try to tackle all of them at once. Choose one or two to begin with. When you have mastered those, add a few more. Baby steps set you up for victory. Combined with some exercise, you will already be on your way to losing weight. It's as simple as that. Eat less. Weigh less.

In the Jewish religion, a girl at the age of twelve, and a boy at the age of thirteen, become a Bas and Bar Mitzvah, respectively. They are now considered adults which signifies they are responsible for their own actions. Interestingly enough, and I do not believe in coincidence, originally I had listed twelve obstacles. While editing I realized how important it was to add the thirteenth. Children behave at whim and need to learn boundaries. Overcoming the challenges above is taking responsibility and beginning to behave like an adult when it comes to food. Mazel Tov on your coming of age!

Chapter ~ 8 ~

~ It's All in the Mind ~

Positive thoughts produce positive results. What we say in our minds, leads to our mood and to our actions. This practice has shown that we influence our emotions and behavior with this one simple habit. You can do an experiment right now. Recall an unpleasant event in your life. Imagine it in as many details as you can. See it in your mind's eye and then go on with your day. Notice how you feel. Are you a bit down? Do you feel grouchy or unhappy? Now try this. Think about the happiest day of your life. View it in your mind, remembering every amazing component that made you smile. There will be a spring in your step, a light-heartedness, and a more carefree attitude in the ensuing hours.

What we think, we end up believing. Set yourself up for success with the following positive mindsets. Thinking you can achieve a goal is critical to being successful. When you start a sentence with "I can't do that," stop yourself. Begin by thinking, "It's possible," or "I can."

Many overweight people judge themselves as failures. The number on the scale causes a negative image of themselves which is completely *not true*. Do you feel inferior because you are not good at math, are not an olympic level ice skater, nuclear physicist or brain surgeon? Does not excelling at any of these

49

make you think less of yourself? Does it damage your idea of who you are overall? Being overweight does this to us so stop right there! Having a weight problem has *nothing to do with how wonderful a person you are!*

This sometimes leads to giving up in areas that have nothing to do with weight. Time to flip the switch. The most important tool of all is confidence. Just because you have failed at losing weight does not mean you will be a failure in the future or in other areas of life.

We have developed a mindset that hunger is an emergency that must be taken care of immediately. Let's view hunger like things on our to-do list. My linen closet is a mess and I really should Marie Kondo the towels, sheets and pillowcases. Imagine hunger the same way. Push it off just like things on your to-do list! You'll eventually eat much sooner than I'll organize my linen closet. Being an adult means knowing we don't have to satisfy every craving the moment we feel discomfort - the next meal is never more than a few hours away.

Hunger pangs can be real but there is phantom hunger. Phantom hunger is psychological. It originates in your mind, not in your stomach. Because it starts in the mind, no amount of food will fill it. When physical hunger or phantom hunger hits, get busy and before you know it, you will be having your next meal. This too shall pass...

We all want to be thin - *yesterday*. Being realistic is very important here. If you lose too quickly, you are more likely to gain it back. If you lose slowly, you are more likely to keep it off! Be confident that however you are losing - a little more slowly - or more quickly - it's the goal that counts. Expect to plateau - that's part of the beast but just keep going! Do your best and God will do the rest.

Muster up imagery of yourself on the scale at your goal weight. If you were ever at your goal weight before, keep those pictures handy to rev up the excitement of getting there again. Think about the smaller clothes in your closet that you'll fit into again. Do anything and everything that will maintain a positive attitude on this journey!

Chapter ~ 9 ~

~ To Weigh or Not to Weigh ~

While losing weight, the choice to use a scale is very personal. We are all elated when the numbers go down. But there's a catch. What if you have been doing everything right and there is a weight gain? How would you feel? Would you be able to shrug it off and say to yourself that next week you will see a change?

Will you notice that you did drink a lot more the day before or your salt consumption was higher? Are you pre-menstrual and you always gain a few pounds this time of the month? Most of us are so focused on the number that we get upset instead of accepting there may be reasons for a gain. If you feel the need to weigh yourself, do it once a month. That will be a truer and more accurate reflection of your efforts.

Rely on how you feel and how your clothes fit. Are you going down a notch on your belt? Are your skirts a bit looser? Do you feel lighter? Are people paying you compliments? Has anyone said you look slimmer? Notice and be aware of changes in your body without having to weigh yourself.

Sometimes we actually gain weight by building muscle. I had a friend bemoan gaining weight despite her best efforts. She looked slimmer so it didn't make any sense to me. I asked her if she was lifting weights and if maybe she gained muscle. She realized it was because she said, "Didn't think of that! I am down two dress sizes." The number on the scale is not the only measure of success.

I put my scale away years ago. If the scale went down I used that as an excuse to eat more, and if I gained weight, I would be upset and would also eat more. Either way, the scale was my enemy. That being said, it may be your best friend. Do what works best for you!

Chapter ~ 10 ~

~ Focus on the Good ~

Biblical Scriptures are for us to learn life's lessons. Was there always a happy ending? Not necessarily. Look at the Book of Job. He suffered terribly. Job's friends tried to convince him he was being punished because he sinned. Yet Job takes the higher ground steadfast in knowing he is righteous and has faith in God. The conversation at the end of the Book of Job, between him and God, does not end in solving the problem of undeserved suffering. It does show Job's unwavering trust that all God's ways are just and with purpose.

My thoughts were stuck in the negative, paying more attention to my problems than to my blessings. My mind was mostly consumed with the misery of being obese. While others would read enjoyable novels, my stack of books were diet and exercise books. Self-help books were also purchased to learn coping mechanisms other than going to food.

Almost every self-help book suggested starting a gratitude journal. Writing down the blessings in my life made me realize I had way more good than bad. I became aware that I should include God in my journal as every gift is from Him and I was neglectful in acknowledging this fact. Even more so, I learned God knows what is best for me; if I don't have it, God knows I don't need it. That awareness hushed thoughts of wanting things I did not have. Reading my blessings did a one-eighty in my mind. The thoughts of happiness overshadowed my troubles. Feeling better, the need to eat for comfort melted away, as did the pounds.

I now pray to see things through God's lens. I know I have choices and I try to align them with how God would want me to live my life in all situations. This enables me to feel support even if the going gets rough without it turning into "self-pitying-stuff-myself-with-pizza-party."

Disappointments are a huge part of life. I have found the following helpful for dealing with them. Picture little boxes in your brain that hold different categories. A box for your job, a box for your friends, a box for your partner, a box for your children. Then label each one. Take one of those boxes and label it, "Problems." You can get really creative here and even make sub-category boxes. One box can be labeled, "Jealousy," one box can be labeled, "Inadequate," one can be labeled, "Overwhelmed," etc.... Of course, you can create new boxes as life throws new curve balls.

When an event arouses any of the feelings represented by a box that would lead to eating, imagine you are opening the box labeled with that feeling. Put them in that box and close it. Do not open the box until the need to overeat to deal with the problem passes. Only when calm, may the box be opened. Now you have put space between the initial anxiety and can calmly discuss the issue with God. Ask for His advice. "What should I do? I am upset about _____."

Talk it out in great detail with God. You may not hear an answer but you should

certainly have diminished the angst to a level where you can control your

emotions and not use food as comfort. Instead, you are going to God for

comfort. He doesn't have any calories. Not even one!

Focus on the good. When your thoughts wander to anything negative, just stop

right then and there. Pick one blessing in your life and start thinking about

that! Pick up your cell phone and call a friend. Look at photos of loved ones, a

gorgeous landscape of flowers that you've taken pictures of. Look at anything

that makes you happy. Write down a list of things that make you smile and

keep that list handy. You can't have two thoughts at the same time. So choose

to be happy!

Chapter ~ 11 ~

~ Does Food Make You Happy or Sad ~

The emphasis on food is astounding. There are more take-out places, restaurants, pizzerias, and coffee shops than ever before. There are food vendors on metropolitan street corners; hot dog carts, gyros, ice-cream trucks - food is everywhere. Scrumptious meals are advertised on billboards. Everywhere we go, no matter if we leave our house or not - we are bombarded with food.

The obsession with food nowadays is not normal. I don't remember cooking shows years ago. On Netflix alone, there is Nailed It, The Chef Show, Chef's Table, Ugly Delicious, Waffles + Mochi, Nadiya Bakes, Best Leftovers Ever, Salt Fat Acid Heat, Zumbo's Just Desserts, The Curious Creations of Christine McConnell, Cray Delicious, The American Barbecue Showdown, Cooked with Cannabis, just to name a few. The number of food posts on Social Media sites is mind-boggling. The photos of the variety of foods and recipes for food is beyond what anyone would have imagined a generation ago.

Food *is* good - back in the day when food was closer to what God intended food to be. We need food to survive. We need to nourish our bodies with the food's nutrients and vitamins that our bodies process through the digestive process. However, all the advertising has glorified food beyond what it is meant to be.

Of course, food should be delicious and satisfying. But too much is out of whack in the way we associate with food in today's world. Back to Social Media, can we see an Instagram post without pictures of what people had for dinner? Can we watch an influencer without them videoing themselves stopping off to buy an iced coffee or fro yo? These postings have made us come to believe that food makes us happy. Everyone eating and drinking is broadly smiling and what I really don't get, is how many of these young ladies are rail-thin and seem to be constantly eating or drinking, let alone eating almost every meal in a restaurant. The two just don't jive as meals prepared at home are usually much lower in calories. We think we are missing out on something if we don't stop at the fast-food drive-through, coffee shop or cafe on the way home from work or errands. We incorrectly believe these make us happy because we see food being enjoyed almost everywhere we turn! It has become so glamorized that the idea of making a coffee at home seems old-fashioned!

Fast forward to the end of the day when you are lamenting and regretting those stops on the way home. "Did I really need to eat all that even though I knew a delicious dinner was waiting for me? Was it really pleasurable?" Or how about the next morning on the scale? Slapping your head, literally, when you see the higher number, you ask yourself, "What was I thinking? Of course the scale went up. I know it was because of the fat-laden, salt-filled, extra calories that I picked up and ate on the way home from work."

We really need to sum up this chapter with two simple questions. Does food make you happy or sad? Do you want food more than you want to be healthy and at your ideal weight? Keep things simple with these two questions in mind. This may be a light-bulb moment that never occurred to you. Ask yourself, "Do I want the piece of cake or do I want to maintain my weight?" Depending on your prior day or even prior week, or possibly what does the week ahead look like, make your decision. If you already ate more than usual, answer "No" to the cake. If you know you are going on vacation the next week and will be eating more than usual, again, say "No" to the cake. If you say "Yes" to the cake, now ask yourself, "How will I feel after I eat it?" Will you be happy or sad?

Relating food to being happy or sad is important. Food should be enjoyable. We should never eat in a way that afterward, we find ourselves miserable. When you make the decision of what to eat, make it a choice, that leaves you without guilt or negative emotions. You can then be happy and enjoy eating that piece of cake.

Remember to ask, "Will it make me happy or sad?" Weigh and measure your decision, with no pun intended, the psychological impact of your choice. Make the choice that will keep you happy and the scale steady.

Chapter ~ 12 ~

~ Prayer and Food ~

In television shows years ago, a scene would depict a family sitting around their table saying Grace before the meal. It is a wonderful idea and doesn't necessarily have to do with religious practice if you object to that. Other religions have a prayer after meals. Some have prayers before and after!

No matter what religious practice you have regarding praying to God before you eat, are you doing it out of habit? Do you actually pay attention that you are talking to Him? I was guilty of rattling off words before eating without paying attention to Whom I was praying. It's quite remarkable how when we do something so often, we do it in such a robotic fashion.

Slow down and pay attention. I now sit when I say my prayer before eating. It forces me to focus on the food in front of me. It's all about consciousness. Take in your surroundings. Turn off the cell phone. Turn off the radio. Put away the newspaper, magazines and any other distractions. If you are not a prayer person, say thank you to the food in your own words. Whichever way and to whom your words are addressed, acknowledge that you are about to eat. Fill yourself with gratitude that you have food. Think about all the steps involved in getting the food to your plate. See everything in front of you instead of fork-to-mouth without a thought about what you are doing. Imagine the food releasing nutrients in your body. Sometimes my prayer as I am eating is asking God to have the food target my personal nutritional needs, even if that food doesn't really have those benefits. Be creative, because God can do anything!

While you are eating, notice the temperature of the food, the texture, the smells and the taste. Notice which side of your mouth you automatically go to when chewing different foods. We have approximately 8,000 taste buds in our mouths; mostly on our tongue. Every area can detect all tastes - bitter, sweet, sour and salty but some flavors are enhanced in particular areas. It is interesting to pay attention and if you are prone to chewing salty foods on one side of your mouth, switch to the other side and notice how different the same foods taste. The difference can be very subtle. The object of doing this is to fully experience and enhance the enjoyment of your meal. The fuller and richer the awareness, the more satisfied one becomes. Stop at this point and thank God, articulating in great detail which tastes you prefer most. Discuss everything you can think of regarding all you are blessed to have on your plate.

At the end of the meal, notice how satisfied you are and thank God for that. Thank God for how fortunate you are to have had the money to buy the food. If your religious practice has an after-the-meal prayer in a foreign language, take the time to look up the meaning of even just one sentence so you can know what you are saying. Knowing the meaning will bring your satisfaction to a higher degree. Your satiation will not only be physical but beyond that to a spiritual encounter resulting in a higher satiety level overall.

Oftentimes, I wonder how I lived before having my day filled with conversations with God. I reflect that I must have been sleep-walking through life, performing my daily activities with such rote, that I never really felt anything. Opening your mouth to speak to the One that created you, ends up enveloping and enriching all of your life. The fact that you are learning to speak to God for help with food will undoubtedly become so habitual that it will extend to talking to God in general.

How fantastic and enriching *all* of your life will be! Everything will be more noticed and more fully experienced. Reminds me of the time I went to France. Being an American, and living in a society where everything was becoming larger, including portion sizes, I was taken aback when served a piece of cake at a patisserie in Paris. To my American eyes, it looked like two bites worth. Even the coffee. About three sips! It all made sense when I went clothing shopping and the largest size was quite small! But this is their secret. Everything was bursting with flavor. The two bites were so filling. The few sips were so satisfying. When you are served such a small but delicious portion, you savor each bite and each sip. Reject shoveling food into your mouth. Eating less and chewing slowly will automatically have you feeling full sooner.

Let's expand our attention when eating and include rich conversations with God, foregoing rich food! As opposed to the smallness of portions in Paris, here we need more - more words - more verbosity - more energy and time (but not more food...) That will lead to a more modest life with simpler activities becoming fulfilling. The need to run and do, buy and possess, will diminish too because so much less will be required to become satisfied in all areas of life.

Chapter ~ 13 ~

~ The Five Senses ~

Our five senses and the organ connected to each one, gives us a glimpse of how each one relates to our experience with food.

1) Sight/Eyes

2) Smell/Nose

3) Hearing/Ears

4) Taste/Tongue

5) Touch/Skin

When Adam ate from the Tree of Knowledge, most sources say he ate an apple. When most of us "sin" with food, we are not bingeing on apples. The idea of not being able to resist food - that is what we are trying to investigate here. Imagine walking into the Garden of Eden. Imagine seeing the only tree God told you not to eat from. When you want to cajole a child to do something, just tell him he's not allowed. That's the fastest way to get them to do it!

How old was Adam when he was created? Wasn't Adam an adult? Shouldn't he have been able to resist? Experience should have taught us that what is forbidden, is most probably something that is not good for us. As a child, we are taught to cross the street at the corner and preferably with a traffic light because it is for our own safety. However, even when we know something is not good for us, there is a sense of adventure in defying reason and solid advice. Even the smartest person, in one split second, can act on impulse. That piece of child is deep inside us waiting to misbehave. The moment something is forbidden we desire it even more!

Our five senses stimulated simultaneously can make a desire more formidable and more difficult to overcome. "Out of sight, out of mind," is truly what happens with food. If we don't see it, we may not remember it's behind a pantry door. In the case of Adam, all his five senses were activated. What was forbidden was in his sight and on his mind! Adam saw the tree full of delicious apples. Have you ever been to an apple orchard? The smell is wonderful! Now just imagine a human being planted an apple tree. As great as that tree could be, *this* tree of apples that Adam had to resist had been directly created by God Himself! You can just imagine how incredible that tree must have smelled, how perfect, how appealing, how tempting! Even the bark of the trees smelled and tasted like the fruit it bore.

Summarizing so far we have the senses of sight and smell activated. Next, we learn that Eve spoke to Adam, offering him a bite of the apple. Next, she pushed Adam and he touched the tree. He saw the tree, smelled the apples, heard Eve's voice and touched the tree. Adam buckled from four senses being activated; seeing, smelling, hearing and touching the tree.

Applying the above to ourselves, we pass a fast food store or a restaurant. The smell of delicious food wafting through the air activates our salivary glands. We peek into the store window and see diners eating sumptuous food. We try to resist going inside, telling ourselves we will just peruse the menu to see what they have for the future. Then we remember there is nothing prepared at home for dinner, so we buy a meal. Unpacking the steaming hot delicious food at home - we lose control and eat it right then and there, not taking the time to plate it or sit down at the table to eat like a normal person.

It was too overwhelming to resist. We saw the food, we smelled the food and we touched the food. The message here is to not fall prey to having too much to resist. If you pass the same restaurant every night walking from the train station to your house, with the delicious smells wafting in the air, and you inevitably can't resist, walk down another street! Even if it means walking a few extra blocks, which is a good thing anyway.

If you know your friend only serves very fattening foods when you are invited for an occasion, simply tell her you are not available but can join for dessert. Show up with a fruit platter and place it down in front of yourself. Alternatively, offer to bring a few healthy options for the meal. The worst thing you can say is that you are on a diet and you need to bring your own food. I remember people telling me, when I stupidly said I was dieting, "Just enjoy yourself this one time." Someone even reacted negatively, accusing me of criticizing the way she cooked. "My food is not fattening. Of course you can eat what I make. Do you think my food is swimming in fats and unhealthy ingredients?" You can't win. You never know how people will react. So offer to cook something. It is always acceptable to show up with a dish or two.

Many challenges create the same situation Adam fell prey to in the Garden of Eden. If going to a movie theater means not being able to resist purchasing popcorn and Milk Duds, go with a friend who never eats at the theater. Or rent the movie and watch it at home with air-popped popcorn sans the butter. Assess the situations you are going into and be creative!

Until you get a handle on overeating, you can choose not to put yourself in difficult situations. Stop yourself from putting others first. How can I insult my parents, my in-laws, and my siblings by not accepting a holiday invitation? What you must know is that you do *not* need to make excuses. You can simply say you are grateful for the invitation but you can't make it. If you start with any excuse, they will come up with all sorts of reasons why you should come. Especially if you say you are on a diet, forget it! You have to learn to put yourself first.

Do not beat yourself up wishing you had more control; eventually, you will.

Even first man couldn't resist.

Chapter ~ 14 ~

~ The Blame Game ~

Babies intuitively know when to stop eating. They will not open their mouths for another spoonful when they have had enough. They will twist their little heads from side to side, mouths zipped shut. So why are we seeing so many overweight children?

There are many causes that factor into the childhood obesity we witness today. We have become a society that eats more take-out and restaurant meals than ever before. These meals are much larger than normal portions. If you were served a normal-sized meal, you would complain. Imagine if you were served four ounces of protein, half a cup of rice or potatoes and a full cup of vegetables. On a dinner-sized plate, the portions would look meager. Getting our "money's worth" has come before getting our "health's worth." You would be appalled if you took a measuring cup to a restaurant and measured how many cups of pasta you are served. For example, a normal portion for a side dish of carbohydrates is half a cup; for a meal, it would be a full cup. In a restaurant, you are probably getting at least two to three cups of rice or pasta, plus the creamy, high-calorie sauce. Portion control is a must in controlling weight, and we are sorely lacking in this area.

Years ago you would rarely see someone snacking as frequently as we do now. We have so many stimuli visually for food that it is hard to keep our minds off it. As mentioned in a previous chapter, we are more food-oriented than ever before in the history of mankind. It's no wonder we aren't heavier than we are. Imagine back in the olden days when you had food for just a few days. Hard to imagine having a small amount of rice, beans and flour that would last a short time before becoming spoiled or full of insects. My mom recalls that as a child one potato would feed her, three siblings and her mother. Without food in a pantry, they never knew if there would be enough food the next day.

Sometimes our advances do not serve us well. The sheer amount of food at our disposal sets us up for eating too frequently and in portions that are too large. We keep too much food in our homes and in our pantries. We cook too much food to begin with and have more than enough to polish off several hundreds of extra calories as we clean up after meals, sometimes totaling more calories than we ate sitting down.

God does not want us to be gluttonous, gorging ourselves till we have to loosen our belts. Wedding celebrations today are out of control. The smorgasbords have meat carving stations, sushi, an array of trays of hot dishes in rich sauces, breads and rolls piled high. The abundance and variety of food is mind-boggling. After the wedding ceremony, we are served a four-course meal and then a Viennese table with desserts. If that isn't enough, there are cookies to go as you wait for the valet to bring you your car.

This is not normal. In addition to overeating being unhealthy, it most certainly would fall into the category of being prohibited in many religions. Gluttony, excessiveness and gorging on food are certainly to be frowned upon. Too much of anything is not healthy. The more you have, the more you want until there is almost no way to be satisfied. Middle of the road is the safest approach when it comes to most things in life. It applies to food as well.

Next time you are in a situation where you indulged in the past, stop for a moment and ask God for help. Ask Him to help you remember how you felt after indulging. Remember the regret, seeing vividly how tight your belt or your dress became, your stomach extended. Now imagine carefully choosing moderate portions of your favorite foods, eating them slowly and savoring every bite. Now imagine yourself home later that day knowing you were in control, your belt fits the same as it did when you left the house hours earlier, your stomach still flat in your dress. Is indulging ever really worth it?

In many religions, there are guidelines to follow. They range from never eating meat, abstaining from food for specific hours of the day, fasting, avoiding pork and lard, not eating leavened bread, abstaining from alcohol, and only eating meat on certain days to name a few. Would anyone think of breaking these rules? The mindset that overeating is breaking the rules in the eyes of God helps us to eat in moderation knowing it is in line with the way we are intended to eat.

Emotional emptiness, boredom, lack of feeling in control - there are numerous reasons for overeating. The problem is that most often there is a lack of awareness in all of these instances. For example, after an argument or a stressful day, somewhere along the way, turning to food to reduce anxiety, became a habit. When and how it started is a mystery as the focus is only on the eating itself and not on any other component. The search for a new diet to lose weight becomes the laser focus rather than what truly needs to be addressed - the circumstances that led to overeating to begin with!

When our lives are more in order, our food is more in control. The word control is a major component here as it is ultimately true that when we are in control of our lives, we are in control of our food and vice versa. If things are steady and manageable, the gut instinct to grab food will fade away. When we are organized and not frantic, food management becomes easier. Remember, failing to plan is planning to fail. When we have more time on our hands and less stress in our lives, it is easier to prepare healthy meals and eat for physical nourishment rather than emotional fulfillment. Ultimately, intuitive eating, relying solely on internal hunger and satiation cues, will again become the norm.

Chapter ~ 15 ~

~ The Biggest Win ~

The biggest win is to be upset and *not* go to food for comfort. Instead, go to God. Here is an example in the Jewish Bible where we are crying out to God in times of need. In Numbers 20:16 it says, "We cried to God who heard our plea." Here is validation that it is okay to "kvetch" (complain) to God when we need His help. This is a perfect example of remembering that there is nothing too small or insignificant to talk to God about. We should never feel we are bothering Him. The truth is God eagerly waits to hear from all of us.

What's your unique language? What would you say to God when someone upsets you? What would you say to God if you got fired from your job? What would you say when someone insults you straight to your face? What would you say to God if someone purposely undermined you? What are the words you would use when asking God to stop you from bingeing? I healed my food addiction remembering to go to God with all my problems, ranging from the seemingly most insignificant to major issues.

That first bite is the most critical one to avoid. Years ago I posted a "Stop" sign on the outside of a kitchen cabinet. It was where I kept snacks for my family. I needed the visual reminder to start talking to God. When I spoke to Him, sometimes just seeing that sign and verbalizing, "God, stop me!" was enough. Sometimes I needed a lot more. God was nudging me to speak to Him at greater length and with more detail. Those few simple words, "God stop me," or "God help me," were no longer enough to stop me from overeating. Just like a muscle in our body, needing to add more weight to achieve the same benefit, that sentence screamed for expatiation. I needed to add to my repertoire to achieve the same outcome, just like a bodybuilder needs to add more weights for improved results. What was required of me now was to speak at length and in greater detail.

My pleas became specific, "God, I want to eat the ice cream in the freezer, but please stop me." That helped more than the simple, "God help me." As time went on, my words became even lengthier, "God help me not eat the ice cream from the freezer because I am anxious and I don't know why, but please stop me now!" It became more natural as if I was talking to a friend standing right in front of me.

Then it changed up again. I started thanking God when a binge was averted. Not only did I ask God before a binge to stop me but I realized I needed to add gratitude afterwards for not bingeing. "Thank you so much for Your help!

Thank you for stopping me from eating the ice cream. Thank you God! Help me identify where this urge to eat is coming from because I certainly am not physically hungry!" "God, You have helped me stop in my tracks many times before when the sudden urge to binge hit me! I can remember hundreds of times, if not thousands when I wanted to eat and I asked for Your help. The pull to eat is so strong and I can't resist without You by my side. God please help me as You have in the past. Please help me not eat out of any need other than nutritional."

Gratitude, more words and lengthier conversations should become as natural as speaking to a friend. The longer one stays with this, the more likely success will ensue. Really understand the joy that will be yours when you walk away from a binge, with God's help. Stopping that desire to eat for comfort is a great win and truly a gift from God. It is almost as if He is right there, with you in your time of need. It is a real high without drugs, medication or food!

Other wins were overcoming the obstacles described in Chapter 7. Every time you accomplish any of the obstacles, give God a great big thank You! Success is something we may have worked hard to achieve, in any area, but let's never forget that God was right there rooting for us, no matter what we are accomplishing.

Not eating at night was the last of the challenges I needed to overcome. It was such a habit that I ate even if I wasn't hungry. When I go through an entire evening without taking a snack, that is time for me to say, "Thank you God. I know that because I requested help from You, that is the only reason I was able to overcome this obstacle."

Sincerely try the conversations described above from the bottom of a broken, humble heart. The more broken and the more humble, the more God will see you need His help. He loves you more than anything and wants to be there for you. But just like sitting around and waiting for someone to read your mind and help you, learn to ask for help.

I thank God for the help He has given me in overcoming my obstacles. I found that it became easier and easier to remain steadfast with my changes when I continued to be thankful. It is a matter of being grateful on a daily basis. Kind of like the adage, "Out of sight, out of mind." Here it is, "Out of awareness, out of mind." It is not easy but vigilance and stick-to-itiveness certainly pay off. You wouldn't slack off in another situation in life where you have worked hard to achieve results and it is the same here.

Saying thank you never loses its appeal. It is human nature that by thanking someone even for the smallest things, they will be reinforced to continue doing what you thanked them for! Not to be misunderstood; God does not need our thank you. We are the ones who benefit because being grateful makes us happier.

Taking this a step further and understanding our connection to God and food, there are days when we are commanded to fast. Their purpose is to connect us to God by removing the human need for food so we become more spiritual, focusing only on our connection to God. We also expunge our sins on these days. We ourselves can claim days to fast, not to punish ourselves or to remove our sins but to get closer to God, to become more angel-like. In the section of the Torah named Naso (Number 6: 1-21), we are introduced to a person called a Nazir, who declares his abstention from particular physical pleasures and foods in his quest for holiness. Not that we need to fast, but it is an interesting idea that removing ourselves from food for a set period of time with the intention of getting closer to God, acts as a vehicle to raise a person to a holier level.

Applying that idea of distancing ourselves from food to achieve a higher purpose, certainly fits in with all the ideas we have been discussing. Take a step back, become aware that overeating is abusing the privilege one has to have enough food, and put it into its proper perspective. Yes, we are to enjoy food with the end resulting in satisfying our needs enough, without overindulgence.

Chapter ~ 16 ~

~ Invisible ~

Improper eating is discussed in Rebbe Nachman's book, called "Likutei Maharan." "The desire to eat brings God to be hidden." The impact these words made on me was indelible. It is mind-boggling that the negative impact of improper eating is included amongst all other lofty Godly teachings. It further supports that we are not alone in this struggle.

God certainly was hidden from me, or shall I take responsibility and reframe to say, I put up the curtain and distanced myself from God when I was overly involved in food. I was asleep all through the years of bingeing. How could there have been room for God in those moments? When I started drawing back the curtain and started speaking to God, the eating became less and less. The more I requested help from God, the easier it became to eat in a normal fashion.

Imagine you distanced your best friend by doing something that would make him ignore you. You would do anything to renew the friendship. Invite God back into your life. Remember, He really wants to be there for you. Talk to God in the greatest detail. Tell Him all about the food binges, the inappropriate amounts, closet eating, overeating; all improper eating. Ask Him to help you be rid of this craziness! The more you ask, the sooner your salvation will come.

We have no choice who are parents are nor how they will treat us. We have no choice who our siblings will be or how our relationships with them will play out. We have no control over the people we are destined to meet. Basically, there are way more things in life that happen to us than the things we have control over. In Danielle Steele's book, "Invisible," the main character is a young woman. The way she dealt with a troubled childhood was believing that it was safest to stay invisible. Let's apply this idea to the overweight individual.

There is a push-pull situation where on the one hand an overweight person wants to be seen but on the other, they wish to be invisible. This certainly described where I was for many years. If you are seen, you may have to experience criticism and disgust from others. If you are not seen, then you spare yourself from feeling shame albeit the outcome is living a lonely life. This happened to me during my overweight years. Don't notice me. I don't want to see the look on your face. I don't want to see the disbelief in the expression on your face nor the scowl that speaks louder than words. "Can't you control yourself! How much do you eat to remain that huge? Why can't you eat like a normal person?"

For years, I did not want to leave the house. The self-criticism was probably greater than the opinions others had of me that I imagined. Even though I wanted to hide, I was blessed that I had to get up, get dressed and get out. I dreaded looking through my closet in the morning as I had so few things to wear. Not only that, the outfits that were too small, that I was hoping to fit into once again, far outnumbered those that fit. It was embarrassing to wear the same few garments over and over again. But carpools, grocery shopping for my family and the myriad errands in running a home forced me to go out.

Looking back it was much worse in my mind than in actuality. The desire to be invisible was with me most of the time. I had to attend the Annual Fundraising dinner for our children's school. I was very involved in charitable work, whether working on the seating plan, the centerpieces for the tables, or planning the menu with the caterer. My attendance was not optional. Inevitably, I would be needed for a table setting left out, an issue with the caterer or some other detail that arose the evening of an event. I was blessed to be a mom and had to go to parent-teacher conferences and cheer my children on when they played sports competing with other schools. I thoroughly enjoyed every dance recital and school play. I had no choice if I wanted to be there for my children and my community, which I certainly desired.

On the other hand, I did want to be seen! I thirsted for conversation and friendships just like any normal weight person. I wanted to be included in going out to dinner with friends, going to the movies or any other activities couples did together. I wanted to be invited to meet other moms in the park so our children would have playdates. I innately was a social person and loved socializing.

And yet, I wanted to be seen as someone that needed help. I wanted to be rescued. I played out a scenario in my mind that a slim person would come over to me, sympathize with my being obese and share the secrets to being normal weight. I wanted to scream from the rooftops, "Anyone out there willing to help me? Does anyone want to lock me up and feed me controlled portions? Would you please shop, cook and plate what would bring the scale down to a number recommended for my height and gender?"

Then I would want to be invisible again…. I wanted it both ways. How great it would have been if only I could get a handle on my emotions and feelings. How great it would have been if I understood that most of the fear of what other people were thinking was magnified. Were there the few who had disparaging thoughts about me? Of course! However, those were much fewer than I imagined and those are the type of people that aren't worthy of being anyone's friend anyway.

We are much more than a physical body. Yes, anyone overweight was out of control with food and unfortunately, the world gets to see that. Other addictions are not necessarily visible to the outside world. But remember, you are a wonderful person, with many talents and gifts. We should be seen for what is on the inside. We should be valued just like any other person,

regardless of a number on the scale. It is a blessing that the world does seem

to be moving in that direction.

Chapter ~ 17 ~

~ Messing Up ~

Messing up is part of the human condition. Show me someone who never made a mistake and I will show you a faker, liar, or a martian from outer space who landed while we were all sleeping. We may all play the game in our heads that everyone else is perfect. Perfect lives. Perfect partners. Perfect friends. Perfect house. Perfect children. Perfect job. The list of how perfect other people are is certainly a very long one.

No matter how perfect other people's lives seem to us, ask any psychologist, therapist or doctor about the staggering number of people on anti-anxiety drugs. The numbers today are astonishing. We have become weak individuals who get anxious over everything. Much of this is self-imposed. More than ever, much of it comes from a desire to create perfect lives. However, that is aiming for something that just doesn't exist.

We all have problems and have situations that are challenging. What does this have to do with food? What does all the above have to do with God?

If we messed up we need to talk to God! Wake up and pay attention to your feelings. Talk and talk and vent and vent. Ask Him to help you never again to overeat when you get upset. Ask Him to help you never again overeat when you feel jealous. Ask Him to help you never overeat when you feel your co-worker got the promotion even though you had seniority and certainly deserved it more. Ask Him to help you never again overeat when a close friend gets engaged to an amazing guy and you're still single dreading your next awkward date.

We must learn to never go to food when we mess up. Eating will only add an additional problem. Not only will you have the issue that drove you to eat, but now you will have the disappointment and angst of having overeaten. It's more productive to change our thoughts and think of it not as messing up, but as a learning experience. What did I learn from what just happened? How can I handle the same situation to my advantage the next time? Coming out of a challenging situation with a solution for the future will ensure not going to food for comfort and set you up for success next time you are in a similar set of circumstances.

Ask God for the answers and even have the audacity to ask why you had to go through the experience. Never overeat because you are upset. Go to God straightaway! Ask Him to stop you in your tracks! Ask him to glue those kitchen doors shut. Ask Him to help you remove all the junk food from your house because until now you made excuses that the rest of your family wants those snacks in the house. Make some really silly requests to lighten up your mood.

That alone will reduce the intensity of your feelings, which drove you to reach for food in the first place. The sooner we make ourselves laugh, the sooner we can take a deep breath and start asking God for help. The sooner we get into the habit of using mistakes as learning opportunities, asking God for possible solutions, the sooner we can let go of going to food, hopefully forever, as we keep our connection with God very constant and very strong.

Chapter ~ 18 ~

~ Psalms ~

If you think crying out to God or asking God for help is something new, it is actually something very old. Psalms was mostly written by King David thousands of years ago. In Hebrew, the name of the book is Tehillim, which means praises. The words encapsulate almost every experience and emotion known to man; they praise God and supplicate before Him.

Chapters were also written by Adam, Abraham, Moses, and King Solomon. However, King David was given the credit for compiling and creating one book, as well as writing most of the 150 Psalms, portraying poems, hymns and prayers.

Reciting Psalms is a symbiotic relationship. Our speaking to God is based on mutualism where both partners benefit from the communication. If you are thinking, "I can see how I gain from this connection but what satisfaction does God have?"

The short answer is God created a dwelling place for Himself in this world. We can't begin to attribute human characteristics to God. God does not get lonely, He does not have needs. However, we can appreciate that God enjoys having interconnection with us. We both benefit, so to speak.

93

The Torah refers to the Pentateuch, commonly referred to as The Five Books of Moses; the books of Genesis, Exodus, Leviticus, Numbers and Deuteronomy. These are replete with conversations between God and man.

The first instance of God "speaking" is when He created the world. He spoke everything into existence. Interestingly the Hebrew word to speak is "dibbur." The three root letters of the word are the same as the word "davar," which means a "thing." For instance, God "spoke" the word "shulchan," which in Hebrew is the word for a table. Tables then came into existence. If we could see, on an incredibly high, spiritual beyond-our-understanding level, the Hebrew letters are what the actual table is made of. The letters are floating around and keeping the physical object in existence where we can see and touch that which we experience as being a table, a solid object. The Hebrew letters literally *are* the table.

As challenging as it is for us to stretch our minds to grasp this reality, which seems very unreal to us, learning about the first use of words and their significance, brings us to the human ability to speak. Usually having a dialogue means there is someone physical that we can see with our eyes and they can talk back to us. There is a give and take. It is quite a challenge when we can't see whom we are talking to and we can't hear a reply from them, either, to believe they are truly there. However, before the telephone was invented, do you think anyone would have believed they could talk and be heard by

94

someone not directly in front of them? Yet they do reply on the other end of the phone! Everything is just one degree of separation. Is it possible that eventually we will neither see nor hear but are still communicating with others? Just something to ponder.

Throughout the Five Books of Moses, we learn of the myriad conversations starting with Adam in the book of Genesis. Of course, God does not actually talk but words depicting human speech are used to describe God talking to bring it down to our level so we can have a glimpse of understanding the communication between God and man. Additionally, the conversations we read about are described as man receiving "Ruach Hakodesh," or experiencing words from God in a dreamlike state. The literal translation of "Ruach" is wind or a breeze; "Hakodesh" means something of holiness. When we hear, the words are carried through the air as sound waves. Ruach Hakodesh, what holy people in the Bible "heard," fits right into this definition. The words are holy words from God floating to them in a surreal way.

Think deeply about this. When things are going well, we believe everything is happenstance. Self-aggrandizement may also result under these circumstances leaving no room for reaching out for help. When we erroneously think our success comes from our own efforts and talents, there would not be any reason to ask for help or be grateful to anyone else but ourselves. Funny how the moment things go wrong, the majority of humankind would cry out, as a knee-jerk reaction, "God, help me!"

Certainly, if God did not want to hear from us, we would never be given any challenges whatsoever. The fact that He created lack in this world is proof positive that He wants to hear from us. Our three forefathers were purposefully given tests to overcome; some were quite daunting! Three things come to mind. Firstly, they inherently felt the need to turn to God for guidance. Secondly, the strength to overcome seemingly insurmountable difficulties could only be achieved with the support of the Almighty. Thirdly, they understood their difficulties were custom-tailored for them to achieve their highest selves.

Beseeching God is in many chapters of Psalms. The verbiage is greatly diverse and the experience of man needing to connect to God is peppered throughout. The words fluctuate between calling or crying out to God, as in Chapter 3, verse 5, "With my voice I call out to God," Chapter 17, verse 6, "I called upon You," and Chapter 30, verse 3, "I cried out to my God," and verses supplicating that God should answer man's prayers; Chapter 4, verse 2, "Answer me when I call out to You," Chapter 17, verse 6 continued, "...so that You would answer me," Chapter 27, verse 7, "Be gracious to me and answer me."

In light of the above, perhaps you may still feel uncomfortable and not yet ready to talk to God. Maybe reciting Psalms, especially the verses denoting conversing with God, maybe the bridge to eventually talking to God in your own words. Consider picking up Psalms, opening to a random page, and reading

King David's words. Just like anything new that is uncomfortable at first, finding

a temporary alternate avenue, could eventuate in speaking naturally to God, in

your own words.

Chapter ~ 19 ~

~ What Do I Eat ~

What do I eat? That's a great question I still have in the back of my own mind every time I see a slim person! What do people eat when they naturally maintain a normal weight without ever having had to consider what or how much to eat!

My fervent goal for this chapter is for you to never have to think about dieting again. I want to share how I learned to eat intuitively. I pray that choosing your meals will be a matter of good habits and overall knowledge about food, without having to think about portions, food groups or calories ever again.

First, back to God. I recommend eating what God created, not what man manufactures. God's food is packed with nutrients. Is there any food God made that would lead you to a binge? Is there any food God made that you would consider overeating? Have you ever eaten apples, oranges, lettuce, cucumbers, or chicken until you were stuffed? You may say to yourself you could eat a cow, but even a steak. Yes, that might be one example where you may eat too much, however, that is not the cause of obesity. The cause of obesity is the processed foods, frozen foods, and foods with refined flour. Reducing these foods is crucial to losing weight and so is eliminating all kinds of sugars, even zero-calorie artificial sweeteners.

Why give up food God did not create? The answer is to get your palette readjusted to knowing what real food tastes like. You may argue there are studies that show no deleterious health effects of eating the offending foods I mentioned above. However, eating sugars of all kinds, even zero-calorie sweeteners, stimulate the brain to crave more sweet foods. Additionally, most are made of chemicals. Bottom line - we want to ingest only real, whole foods. Become a very careful label reader and ditch foods with sugar, artificial sweeteners, refined flours, preservatives and artificial food coloring.

Very helpful to losing weight is limiting simple carbohydrates which includes white bread, bagels, pretzels, cookies, cakes, cereals, etc... Even as early as 1951, Raymond Greene (1901-1982) wrote in his book "The Practice of Endocrinology - A Diet for Obesity," "Foods to be avoided: 1. Bread, and everything else made with flour. 2. Cereals, including breakfast cereals and milk puddings. 3. Potatoes and all other white root vegetables. 4. Foods containing much sugar. 5. All sweets. You can eat as much as you like of the following foods: 1. Meat, fish, birds. 2. All green vegetables. 3. Eggs, dried or fresh. 4. Cheese. 5. Fruit, except bananas and grapes."

Interesting! Since then so much time has been wasted doing study after study on every different food group, many 'new' diets and diet theories to come along and all with conflicting results. The real conclusion is that all are temporary fixes without sustained results.

Keep it simple. Listen to Dr. Raymond Greene; take his advice which jives with eating what God made. The closer to these foods, the fewer ingredients, the easier it will be to have your body achieve its genetically programmed healthy weight. Barring any medical reasons not to, wine (not sweet dessert wine), may also be enjoyed, (but do check with your doctor first). It does not raise insulin or impair insulin sensitivity; yeast consumes the sugar in the grapes. Your diet may include small amounts of minimally processed foods with as few ingredients as possible.

Intermittent fasting is all the rage now and is highly touted as having health benefits in addition to weight loss. Speaking from a personal viewpoint, I would say to cautiously approach this new technique. As someone who had been obese and went through years of failed dieting, I am concerned that prolonged hours of not eating could lead to bingeing. Therefore, I hesitate to recommend and have strong reservations, but again, there is no "one-diet-fits-all," and intermittent fasting may work for you. Again, ask your doctor first!

Unfortunately, our society has moved away from foods that God made. Mankind survived for thousands of years on fruits, vegetables, seeds and nuts for snacks. How many friends admit that fresh fruits and vegetables rot in their refrigerator bins? We are not in the habit of reaching for these foods but rather for the cookies or chips, claiming we don't have time to start washing and peeling.

It is hard not to pick up a magazine without an article touting the latest and greatest advice on how to lose weight. When I was young, I would voraciously read every single one I could get my hands on, hoping to find the secret to getting and staying slim. I don't remember how old I was when I realized nothing new was ever being said. It was all the same old advice over and over again until one day, I did read an article that was super helpful! The article was titled, "The Fridge Diet." The advice in that article was so simple yet so effective.

The gist of the article ties right into Adam in the Garden of Eden. What we see is what we desire. How many of us put our fruits and vegetables in the fruit and vegetable bins? We all do! They are specially designed to regulate temperature and humidity levels, to keep them fresh for a longer period of time. Now at the risk of spoiling faster, this article recommended storing fruits and vegetables at eye level. I will add to this efficacious advice. Wash and prepare the fruits and vegetables and store them in see-through containers. Amazing! Next time you open the refrigerator, the bright colors of the red peppers, the dark leafy greens, the orange cantaloupe, the purple grapes - they will be right in front of your eyes. You will automatically reach for those health-enhancing foods. And they won't be left to rot in the opaque bins! I practice what I preach. There is a bowl of washed apples in my fridge and a glass container of washed peppers, carrots and cucumbers. Set yourself up for success by being prepared.

Your diet should consist of whole foods. Foods that have minimal processing. The closer to the shaft of wheat, the better the bread. Again, as in any food, bread should have few ingredients. I read an interesting study that explained why a majority of adults in our generation need their wisdom teeth pulled. Years ago when people ate apples and nuts for snacks, real whole grain bread, they needed more teeth to chew their food. Studies have shown that our jaws are smaller and can no longer accommodate 32 teeth as the foods we eat today are so processed and soft. We grew up on soft white bread rather than whole grain which requires a lot more chewing!

I recommend discussing with your medical practitioner any diet you decide to follow. Below is a very general list of suggested foods to eat. I am not giving amounts as they vary from person to person but a broad outline of daily nutritional needs across all food groups.

Salad and Raw vegetables: These are the foods that I savor the most. There are so many lettuces nowadays. Choose from romaine, baby butter, mesclun and dark-leafy greens such as arugula, spinach and kale. Iceberg seemed to be the only lettuce available when I was growing up! The deeper the color, the more nutrients. Add raw pepper, a little chopped red onion, cucumbers, tomatoes, sprouts, radishes and carrots. Get creative!

Try something new! I love snacking on raw jicama, raw cabbage chunks, raw parsnips and raw kale, raw broccoli florets and raw celery. These are all great chopped up and combined with leafy greens, cucumbers, tomatoes, string beans, and zucchini.

Cooked vegetables: Broccoli, cauliflower, string beans, mushrooms and peppers are my personal favorites. These have so few calories and are particularly low in carbohydrates that you can eat generous portions while losing weight. Sweet potatoes, yams, carrots and winter squashes are higher in carbohydrates so be mindful of their portion size. I love to roast almost every vegetable! Did you know that frozen vegetables are considered to be as healthy as fresh because they are flash-frozen. When you buy frozen vegetables there is a short window of time from when the vegetable is picked till it is frozen. When buying fresh ones, you may be buying vegetables that are days from being picked and may be sitting on the shelf for several days before you purchase the them.

Protein: Chicken, turkey, beef, fish, eggs and beans. The simpler they are prepared the better. Must I say do not fry or smother in high-calorie fatty sauces? A spray of herb infused oil with some salt and pepper, balsamic vinegar, mustard, a thin layer of avocado mayonnaise with some spices are all most proteins need to be flavorful. If you prefer cooking in a sauce, a sugar-free marinara or tomato sauce with vegetables simmered in a pot is also a great way to cook protein. As for beans, make sure to soak overnight before cooking. Adding a small piece of kombu (a sea vegetable) while cooking helps reduce the gas in the beans.

Fats: Avocado oil is the safest when cooking with high heat. Extra-Virgin first cold-pressed olive oil is also a good choice. Organic butter, seeds, nuts and avocados fall into this category. I choose a high-quality avocado-based mayo when using mayonnaise. I particularly like Sir Kensington Vegan Mayo, Sir Kensington Avocado Oil Mayo, Chosen Foods Avocado Mayonnaise and Bragg's salad dressings.

Whole Grains: Quinoa, millet, buckwheat, brown rice, farro, barley and slow-cooked steel cut oatmeal, whole grain bread (rye, pumpernickel). Whole grain should be the first ingredient when purchasing bread. Sourdough bread is an excellent choice. Have the bakery slice the loaf for you as the crust is very hard and store it in the freezer. Make sure they do not add honey or sugar. True sourdough bread will not have these added. Do be mindful that these are high in carbohydrates and should be eaten in moderation.

Dairy: Plain yogurt, cottage cheese, shredded cheese, feta cheese, and milk. When choosing dairy, it is best to buy the middle-fat content choice as full-fat simply has too much fat and calories while fat-free is higher in sugar content. The label should read lower-fat, low-fat or reduced-fat.

Fruits: All fruit is wonderful. Berries, melons, apples, oranges, bananas, mangoes, grapefruits, persimmons, etc. All fruit is zero points on certain weight-loss programs. However, know yourself, because of the sugar content in some fruits, is it prudent to limit them due to certain medical conditions. Ask your health practitioner how many fruits a day are best for you.

To pack the most nutrients into your diet, you should have a wide variety of colors on your plate. The more colors the better as each color represents different vitamins and minerals! I recommend starting a meal with a raw salad. Your dinner plate should be divided in half. One-half should be your cooked vegetables. The other half should be divided in half; one-quarter of the plate for each portion. One-quarter should have your protein and the other quarter your carbohydrate. No measuring, no weighing. It shouldn't take that much effort to eat properly! Don't use huge plates. As you lose weight, you may need less food. If you are of smaller stature, consider using a salad-sized plate instead of a dinner plate. You can always take some more if you truly are not satisfied.

I know there are times when we just don't feel like cooking or preparing even the simplest meals. I will open a can of beans (chickpeas are great - you can throw them into the toaster oven and bake with spices), or canned fish and add to a salad. I recommend the following brands of canned fish: Wild Planet, Trader Joe's, Safe Catch, Vital Choice and Natural Catch. As I mentioned above,

Eden brand is my preferred brand of canned beans as they soak their beans and cook with kombu which lessens digestive issues, as mentioned before.

What about dessert? Fresh fruit is best. I do live in the real world and sometimes a piece of fruit won't be satisfying. So occasionally, here are some additional options below:

Chocolate: Choose the highest percentage of cocoa in the chocolate bar your taste buds would enjoy. Only consume those sweetened with natural ingredients or Stevia. Better yet, enjoy chocolate-covered nuts. Remember. Slow down. Sit down. Enjoy! Hu Kitchen is the chocolate I personally eat - all their products, including their chocolate-covered nuts are excellent.

There are companies that make healthier options for chips, popcorn and crackers. Look for chips made from vegetables such as plantains and beets. Look for organic and those made with higher quality oils like avocado or extra virgin olive oil. Stay away from rice flour, potato flour and potato starch! Read the ingredients. I recommend these: Terra chips, Skinny Pop popcorn, Skinny Pop popcorn mini-cakes, Mary's Gone Crackers, Hu Kitchen Grain-Free crackers, Wasa crackers, GG Bran Crispbreads. These items come in different flavors. Try several and rotate which you like best. Variety is great for increasing satisfaction.

Speaking of snacking, when out on the run for an entire day, and there is no time for a meal, I usually bring an apple with a bag of celery and carrot sticks.

Raw nuts are also a good choice. I also recommend the following protein bars

and cookies when I need something non-perishable to throw into my purse.

Mosh Bars, RX Bars, Lara Bars and Blue Mountain Organics 12 Grain Protein

Cookie, to name a few. There are so many great ones on the market, so when

choosing a bar or cookie, purchase the ones with the fewest ingredients. Shy

away from bars with artificial sweeteners or added sugars (brown rice syrup,

Maltitol, anything ending in 'ose.' If there is added honey, maple syrup or agave

- they are better than artificial sweeteners or sugar, but it should not be one of

the first few ingredients). The easiest thing to remember - the bars that have

ingredients you can pronounce are the best ones to buy. That goes for all food!

This list is just to give you ideas when you need to feel what society today calls

a normal snack. Trust me, I know! I was accused of being the "worst mother in

the world." I was so awful because we were the *only family in the entire world*

that didn't have soda in the house. I was the "worst mother in the world"

because I spent hours a week preparing trays of fresh fruits and vegetables for

my children to eat when they came home from school. Everyone else came

home to boxed cakes made with tons of sugar, artificial ingredients and

preservatives. I admit, if that was my crime, I was the worst mother.

Rotate your food, keep variety in your food and maintain portion control. It is

up to you to decide as you are all adults reading this book. Be reasonable. One caveat I should mention now is there are some individuals who do better without variety, at least in the beginning. It is hard for me to cover all bases, meaning all personalities when it comes to a relationship to food. If you fall into this group, and if the same menu day in and out is easier for you to stick to, then do that. Again, this is about finding a plan that works for you as an individual. No one can tell you what keeps you satisfied but as long as it keeps you on track then that is what works best for you.

Additionally, make sure you have several colors of food on your plate. When I coach children on how to eat for health, I print off an "Eat by Color" chart, easily accessible on the Internet. I teach them to check off the box for the color of the foods they have eaten in a day. Then I explain that the more boxes of colors they have checked off, the more vitamins they have eaten that day. Typing this now makes me think adults should do this, too!

Think about a plate with a piece of white meat chicken, iceberg lettuce and steamed cauliflower. You may physically fill up on this meal but I doubt you will leave the table satisfied. Think about the same piece of chicken with a side of purple yam and broccoli. Much more appealing! We talked about using our senses in the chapter, "The Five Senses." Now we are describing becoming satisfied with our meal when we have a visual medley of color. Texture is important, too. Instead of eating a baked potato with steamed vegetables, slice the potato into thin rounds and roast until crispy. Much more satisfying!

Moderation certainly is the key to success in weight loss but more importantly, it is the key to health. Why we have become so far removed from intuitive eating can certainly be blamed on availability and food storage never available before the 1940's or so. Food did not have a shelf life. Bread became stale overnight without preservatives. The refrigerator was not a common household item till about the year 1930. The cupboards were pretty much bare and contained few items. Food in the home included beans, flour, oil, sugar and salt. It took a good amount of time to prepare a meal and food was cooked from scratch.

Of course, food preservatives and refrigeration have helped us in many ways but the downside is how much food we have in our homes and the diminishment in quality. We are surrounded by so many choices, 24/7, that it beckons us as never before. It is always available. It is so easy to pack in way too many calories if there are cookies, pretzels, chips, crackers, cereals, frozen dinners, frozen pizza, etc... available to us in an instant. At least before the invention of the microwave, we had to wait twenty minutes to reheat food from the freezer. Now? The instantaneous access to food has certainly played a role in the battle of weight we see today.

Initially, it will be hard to subscribe to the above recommendations because habits die hard. Begin by getting rid of the foods that challenge you most. You will be doing everyone a favor. Even the slim family members. No one needs to eat unhealthy food.

Eating the food God created is the best way to regulate your weight. Regulating your weight will also help regulate your moods. Eliminating sugar will get rid of those sugar highs which result in a spiraling downward of your mood. All in all, eating healthy only has benefits across the board. And not one single drawback.

Chapter ~ 20 ~

~ Maintenance ~

Weight maintenance is an ongoing, life-long process. You have never "arrived!"
Just last night I had a friend over for dinner. Not your typical, overweight since
childhood friend, but a friend that gained weight in his 50s. This friend was
skinny his entire life. Never once did he have to think about dieting. Never did
he have to make a choice not to eat the third slice of pizza or the huge hero
sandwich from the deli.

I had not seen him for a few weeks since advising him on how to lose weight.
At dinner, I noticed he looked a bit slimmer. I inquired and much to my delight,
he'd lost nine pounds. But then he made a statement that was totally incorrect.
He said, "I am not happy eating this way. I can't wait to go back to my old way
of eating."

The sirens went off in my head. I felt like screaming at him but instead
composed myself. "We need to have a conversation," I told him. I gently
proceeded to explain that the way he will eat when he gets down to his desired
weight, will be very similar to how he is eating now *for the rest of his life.*

It's a fact. Most people regain their weight because they go back to their old eating habits.

Does this make any sense? Of course not! The definition of insanity is doing the same thing and expecting different results! How could anyone think that eating the same way they ate before they lost weight would result in maintaining their weight loss?

To maintain a weight loss you basically should eat the way you have been eating to lose weight. As the scale goes down and our bodies weigh less, we need fewer calories. The variables to know how many calories each person should consume to lose weight can be generalized according to sex, height, weight, age and activity level. Just as there are charts to find an approximate number of calories needed to lose weight, there are charts to give an idea of how many calories are needed to maintain a particular weight.

However, I find charts often end in frustration. "But I am eating the amount of calories the chart says I should eat to maintain my weight yet I am gaining weight!" The difference between men and women, the amount of body fat to muscle ratio, activity level, and genetic make-up; all impact how many calories a person can consume to lose or maintain weight. Science alone has not been able to nail down much when it comes to knowing exactly how many calories and exact activity levels. So again, my advice is to eat similar to the way you were eating while losing weight. Very gradually add more food to your current consumption. As long as the scale stays the same, you can continue to add, albeit in small amounts.

For example, you may want to add a slice of bread every other day or a potato. If the scale stays the same, you are good to add again. The next week you may choose to add a slice of pizza. If the scale stays the same, the next week you may choose an additional food. Be smart and read labels. The portion amount indicated on every Nutrition Fact label is now your best friend. I had a client make the mistake of thinking that four ounces of sweet potato chips was equal to eating four ounces of a baked sweet potato. Sure enough, the Nutrition Fact label showed a portion of only *one ounce* of the sweet potato chips equaled

four ounces of cooked sweet potato, not four ounces of the sweet potato chips!

As I am not a proponent of using the scale for losing weight as discussed in Chapter 9, "To Weigh or Not to Weigh," I am much more in favor of using the scale while trying to find the amount of food you need to maintain your weight. Sometimes we think we are eating only half a cup or four ounces. If you are not maintaining weight, try weighing and measuring for a week. You may be adding a whole cup of pasta when you thought you were adding half a cup. You can fool yourself but you can't fool the scale.

You do need to be more vigilant about keeping track of your weight, but just for a short while. Before you know it, you will intuitively know how much is right for you. You will come to know if you need to cut back by the way your clothes fit or how flat your tummy is, or isn't when you wake up in the morning. You should go to sleep feeling a bit hungry.   You should wake up with an appetite for breakfast. You should be able to get from breakfast to lunch without being hungry as there are usually fewer hours between these meals than between lunch and dinner. Notice if you get very hungry between meals. If you do, add a snack. Getting too hungry may lead to overeating and that is what we are trying to get away from!

Snacks can be important especially if you are very active. So choose your snacks wisely. If you've done a heavy workout with weights, a snack high in protein is in order. It can be a scoop of protein powder or some plain yogurt. Listen to your body!

Get to know your body by relying on your hunger signals. These will be your guide. The more you pay attention and are aware of these signals, the more success you will have. You are worth it. And of course, ask God to help you know the difference between physical and emotional hunger. Ask God if you really need that snack. And if the answer is yes, ask God what your best choice would be. He is there waiting for your questions and ready to give answers.

Being in touch with and very aware of your satiety levels is of utmost importance. Review the strategies to lose weight in Chapter 10 as these will be important for maintenance as well. If I would choose only one as being the most important, I would choose eating slowly. I would also suggest that now that you are slimmer, you do not need as much food. Your stomach is smaller and physically cannot hold as much as before. Remember those people you used to hate who would say, "Oh I can't eat another bite! I am so full!" - now you are one of those people.

Notice that the first few bites of food taste best. Let's play a game. The next time you eat one of your favorite foods, make sure you have a good appetite. Sit down and take a bite. Write down, on a scale of one to ten, the number associated with how delicious that first bite is. One is just okay and ten is wowing your taste buds. Take a second bite. Do the same exercise. Write down a number between one and ten. Do this for as many bites as it takes to heighten your awareness that as we eat more, our tastebuds deaden and do not have the same satisfaction as those first few bites.

Exercise is very important to maintain weight. Remember that muscle burns more calories at rest than fat. Maintaining those muscles will ensure you are burning calories at a sustained metabolic rate. If this sounds daunting, and you question why you still have to put in so much effort, think about any other area in your life. Do you slack off and expect the same results? No! Weight maintenance is no exception. There is still work to do and your attitude is integral to your success.

Focus on staying in the same clothing size. Focus on improved and sustained medical benefits from being at a lower weight. Think of every area in your life that has improved. And if you ever stop for one moment and think you want to throw in the towel, stop and remember how much more miserable you were being overweight.

Chapter ~ 21 ~

~ Did Someone Say Exercise ~

There are many more benefits to exercise besides burning calories. Exercise

benefits the mind, body and soul. I could absolutely cry thinking about the year

I was stuck at a high weight, even though I had already lost fifty pounds. Had I

called the World Book of Guinness Records I may have won the contest for a

person that plateaued for the longest period of time in the history of dieting.

There was not one bite off my food program and I exercised seven days a week,

even when I was sick. The treadmill was my buddy. Aerobic classes on VCR

tapes and long walks were daily.

Frustrated is mild to describe how I felt. Stuck. Fat. Angry. Miserable. Failure.

I could barely think of anything else except hoping the next morning the scale

would budge. And it didn't for an entire year. Streams of tears ran down my

face as I faced another day with zero results for my herculean efforts. Can you

imagine working so hard for so long and coming up empty-handed?

"How could she possibly be dieting and not lose weight with how much she still

weighs? Not possible!" "No way she is exercising as much as she says she is."

When I told a doctor about my efforts, he clearly didn't believe me. He asked,

"Are you on the sea food diet?" I thought he meant fish so I replied that I wasn't. He answered, "Judging by your weight, I believe you are on the 'See food diet,' you see food and you eat it." I wish I could tell you I made up this story for impact in the book, but sadly this really happened to me.

I can see as if it was yesterday people doubting my efforts and not believing it was possible. The walks I took were up and down hills, and steep ones at that. I lived in very hilly terrain and as soon as my youngest child was off on the school bus, my sneakers were on my feet and my hour-long walk began.

I was miserable to the point that even though I had aching knees, blisters on my feet and sore muscles, coupled with many days of being hungry in between meals, the scale didn't budge.

Then I read about weight training. I had never heard of a woman lifting weights before but I was at a loss of what else to do. I joined a gym and hired a personal trainer. I lifted weights three times a week and was sweating bullets by the end of each session, in addition to running on the treadmill or taking a long walk. The scale did not move that first month. I cried to my trainer. How could I have not lost any weight by staying on my food program and adding weight training? He encouraged me and assured me the weight would start coming off. He too was surprised saying I looked thinner but I only measured my success by the numbers on the scale.

Miracle of miracles. After the second month, I lost weight! I began steadily losing weight, with the normal short-term plateaus, even a pound or two gain, and then would continue losing again.

Whatever exercise program you choose, the phrase, "No pain, no gain," does come into play. Set yourself up for success by choosing the type of exercise you like best as those are the ones you are most likely to continue. Combine cardio like walking or running, outside or inside on a treadmill, with lifting weights. The elliptical is a good choice as it is less jarring on the knees. Biking, tennis, pickle ball, ping pong, basketball - anything that gets you moving! Build up slowly, not tackling so much that you wouldn't be able to continue.

Work up to exercising for at least 20 minutes but no more than an hour. Studies show that exercising more does not necessarily aid in losing more pounds nor are there increased health benefits - which is really what this is ultimately all about.

Don't have time to exercise? Stop checking your social media. Think about all the time you spend scrolling through them. Choose one you are willing to give up and there you have freed up at least twenty minutes each day, and when you were probably sedentary.

Get creative in adding additional steps to your day. Park your car several blocks from your destination. If you live within a ten-minute walk from the bus or train you take to work, walk instead of taking the car. Instead of sitting when talking on the phone, pace around your office or your house. When you start to do these small changes on a regular basis, they become a habit. It all adds up.

Make exercise convenient. Leave weights where they are easily accessible, instead of in the basement. Do some bicep and tricep exercises while talking on the phone, and add steps throughout your day. Think of ways you can incorporate movement naturally into your day. Everything adds up burning more total calories.

The following study proves you can fit exercise into the busiest schedules. Both of the following groups insisted they were too busy to fit exercise into their day. Control group A was told to exercise ten minutes, three times a day. Control group B was instructed to exercise thirty continuous minutes per day. After one month, Group A totaled more minutes exercising than Group B. Ten minutes is certainly more manageable whereas half an hour may not be feasible. Additionally, Group A reported exercising more than the ten minutes they planned on doing. They felt so good that they continued for longer and longer periods of time.

Be good to yourself. Make the time to exercise. Start with a few minutes. You will notice that you too will probably extend the time allotted because you will feel so good. The benefits far outweigh any business meeting, commitment you may have made, or any housework that needs to be done. They can all wait. Being in better physical shape will help you accomplish more in less time and with a healthier mental attitude.

Chapter ~ 22 ~

~ Summing it Up ~

Being overweight brings a host of psychological issues including low self-esteem and insecurities. I tried putting it into perspective, and of course, there are much worse things to experience in a lifetime. It still doesn't take away from the suffering of being overweight. I will never know why I was faced with this challenge. The only way to have a modicum of understanding is that this challenge shaped me into the person I was supposed to become.

Looking back, I now look at this as a gift rather than a curse, because turning to God was the result. Had my life gone along swell, I may never have gotten past rote observance in my religion. Hitting rock bottom, coming to a point in life where I saw no way out from being miserable, had me turn to Him. In the end, all I can truly say is, "Thank You." Yes, thank You, with a capital "Y."

How many times in our lives have we experienced something where we could have gleaned great advice but didn't take it to heart or ignored it? How many times have we put blinders over our eyes and not seen what we should have done? There are so many ways God tries to get our attention. There are so many times God was shouting, "Over here. Look no more. Here are all your answers," but for years I looked the other way.

So anytime you are being called by the refrigerator or pantry and feel you don't have enough strength to resist the call of the chips and ice cream, - remember - you may not have the strength alone to resist. You need help just as I still do. Connect to God in your own unique way, asking for whatever help you need.

Admittedly, as this book comes to an end, I initially wrote it to help everyone out there become their best self. The first goal was to become a healthy weight, but it ended up becoming much more so to have a connection to God. Once you have implemented the suggestions in the previous pages, I fervently hope that you will connect to God in every single area of your life down to the smallest detail. I can only imagine that if the whole world becomes attached to a Higher Power, we will live in a world of peace and tranquility. If we all go to God to resolve our issues, wouldn't it be wonderful to be kind, forgiving and embracing each other? Imagine utopia - yes, we can achieve this! Be the first one to grant forgiveness. Try to put yourself in someone else's shoes. And if none of the above works, just accept every relationship for where and what they are. I highly recommend the book by Yehudis Samet, "The Other Side of the Story."

But always remember to say, "God, please help me and God, thank You."

Afterword

As in my first book, "Winning the Weight Loss War, How I Lost 100 Pounds for Good - and How You Can, Too," this was written with one goal in mind; to help others suffering from an addiction. How, what, when and why questions to how one person eats to live but another lives to eat - we can never answer. Studies have proven that putting certain people in a room with tempting desserts will have their mouths watering. It is not in their control. Others are completely not affected one way or the other.

I am in group #1, born to eat and even to this day, I can override my sanity and succumb to food I thought I would never eat again. I am wired this way. Interestingly enough, I recently heard a psychologist say there is scientific evidence proving that through genes, a person is born with fears even from generations ago. They automatically have the same ones a parent or even a grandparent had, without any experiences or circumstances to have induced that fear. Seems this also applies to appetite.

Writing this book was similar to the first. An ardent, and sometimes torturous adventure! It was so hard to get from the feelings to the ideas, to the written words.

While having anxiety from the enormity of writing this book, these texts took place with a dear friend (initials C.F.):

Me: "Remind me - why am I bothering to do this?

Before she can reply, I continue:

~ "I really only want to help other compulsive eaters"

~ "I no longer feel deprived, I want that for others"

~ "I am happier than ever, I want that for others"

~ "Let people know God truly exists and is there for us"

Friend: attached a "heart" emoji to my texts.

Me: "Phew. Thanks for reminding me why I am writing this"

So here we are struggling to overcome addictions; even though this book and my personal struggles were with food. It can rear its ugly head any day and at any moment, but gratefully it is rare as long as I keep up my connection to and my conversations with God. The result is that I am enjoying a much closer relationship with Him. I hope you are enjoying a deeper, more meaningful connection with Him in addition to overcoming compulsive overeating or any addiction.

I also must admit, that if asked, "Would you like to have never had this problem to begin with?" The answer would be a resounding, "Yes." But in the next moment, a resounding, "No,"

130

Acknowledgments

Without God directly handing me my weight struggles, I would have had no reason to write this book. I am so grateful to Him on so many levels.

I am grateful that it gives me something in this world to give back to others. As mentioned in my first book, all the effort is worth it even if I help only one person. I am blessed to have positive feedback of definitely helping more than that! People have come up to me and said, "When you wrote about your struggles and that you ultimately had success, it gives me hope I can also succeed." "Your book made me cry. In a good way." "I loved and really connected to what you spoke about on page 97." All these comments are gifts from God.

I know this was all divinely orchestrated. Every book I read, every class I took, every conversation I have had with people and with God, every single choice I have made in life, every experience and everything I have done, have all led me to write this book. Thank You for squeezing out all You know I can produce. I can only hope and pray and, of course, ask You that this book will help others.

Thank you to my friends who helped edit. Celine, Michla, Beverly, and Ann - I greatly appreciate the time you took and the positive feedback!

About the Author

Rivka Fuchs, AAPC, CMCC, is a certified Life Coach and certified Master Coach and Counselor. She is certified in America and in Israel by Refuah Institute.

She can be reached by email: rivkafuchscoach@gmail.com

Her art can be viewed on Instagram: @rivka_fuchs_art

She enjoys her family and friends. Exercise is very important as is keeping all meals simple.

Made in United States
Orlando, FL
09 December 2024

55301211R00075